DAVID ELLIOT COHEN

THE WRONG DOG

yellow pear press

THE WRONG DOG

For permission requests, please contact the publisher at:
Mango Publishing Group
2850 S Douglas Road, 2nd Floor
Coral Gables, FL 33134 USA
info@mango.bz

For special orders, quantity sales, course adoptions and corporate sales, please email the publisher at sales@mango.bz. For trade and wholesale sales, please contact Ingram Publisher Services at customer.service@ingramcontent.com or +1.800.509.4887.

The Wrong Dog: An Unlikely Tale of Unconditional Love

Library of Congress Cataloging-in-Publication number: 2021949478
ISBN: (paperback) 978-1-64250-899-4, (ebook) 978-1-64250-900-7
BISAC category code: PET010000, PETS / Essays & Narratives

Printed in the United States of America

CONTENTS

1. A NEW PUPPY, PART 1

Way back in November 2000, my future wife Laureen sent her first husband, Guenter, to a well-regarded Labrador breeder with very straightforward instructions: please pick up the eight-week-old female pup that Laureen had selected after weeks of research and more than three months on a waiting list. But Guenter—who's a dashing celebrity chef from Germany's Black Forest and frankly a little bit wild—often flouted instructions. And when he arrived at the breeder's place of business, he was unimpressed with Laureen's selection and smitten instead by a little rough-and-tumble white male with honey-dipped ears and a proud bearing. So true to his Teutonic nature and without any further consultation with Laureen, Guenter swapped her sleepy female for a hyperkinetic, testosterone-infused ball of fur.

Meanwhile, back at the house, Guenter and Laureen's two young daughters—bashful, blonde four-year-old Angela and sweet freckled two-year-old Grace—couldn't wait to meet their new puppy. When they heard Guenter's fire-engine red Porsche roar up the long gravel driveway, they leapt up and down on the gray velvet sofa screaming, "He's here, Mommy! He's here!" And when Guenter strode through the front door bearing the stylish black tote he had acquired just for the occasion, the girls were practically bursting to meet the amiable ingénue whose baby picture they had passed one to the other for weeks. But what they got instead was a frenzied, out-of-control hellion—rolling, yipping, and slip-sliding his way across their slick oaken floor like a tiny Tasmanian devil.

Laureen, a seasoned trial lawyer who tends to maintain her cool even in vexing situations, said as calmly as possible, "Guenter, this is not the puppy we discussed."

"*Ja, ja,*" Guenter replied, "but let me explain…"

Laureen cut him off right there. "Guenter, there were only two females in the litter. Three other families wanted them. And I spent two months, Guenter, two months convincing the breeder to give one of those females to us. I let the breeder inspect our house, Guenter. He made me sit through an interview for Christ's sake."

"*Ja, ja,* I know all that," Guenter replied, still confident for some reason. "But believe me, Laureen, this is a very *gut* dog. He was the biggest puppy in the litter. He is strong and healthy. And he has… how do you say… a very *spirited* personality."

Any further objection on Laureen's part was preempted by the girls' ecstatic reaction to their new puppy's antics.

"I like *this* puppy," Angela declared. And on the spot she named him Simba after the hero of Disney's *The Lion King* movie. Well, she didn't precisely name the new puppy after the lion king. Angela, who even now deplores change of any stripe, actually named him after the family's recently deceased Samoyed, who tragically succumbed to liver cancer at the tender age of four. Samoyeds are big Siberian sled dogs with fluffy white manes. So Simba I actually did look like a lion—or perhaps more accurately an albino lion. Simba II didn't—at least not yet. But despite that quibble, Angela christened the new puppy in his predecessor's memory.

So at the beginning of this story, Simba II was the wrong dog with a secondhand name. Laureen had wanted a sweet, even-tempered female suitable for two little girls and a quiet suburban routine. Simba II, on the other hand, couldn't have been more macho or frenetic. He would have been far better suited to a farm or a cattle ranch or some other outdoorsy situation where his size, strength, and stamina would have made him the ideal companion. But as fate and Guenter would have it, Simba II began his life in a sleek modern house, all done up in black, white, and gray, in leafy Buckhead, Atlanta, with an ambitious hard-working lawyer mom, two pretty little girls, and a rakish Prada-clad chef.

In time Simba II would grow up to be a handsome, robust dog that at ninety muscular pounds was immense for his breed—a Labrador XL we'd call him. And as big as he was, he would have an even bigger head that lent him an air of masculine wisdom. That, combined with his proud carriage and noblesse oblige toward lesser members of his species, would mark Simba II as canine aristocracy—or at least that's how we'd see him. And well down the road Angela's spur-of-the-moment decision to name Simba II after an animal king would seem, if not terribly original, then certainly fitting.

Not for nothing would we someday bestow upon Simba II a string of nonsensical alliterative honorifics. For in our family's opinion, Simba II would indeed become Duke of the Dogs, Lord of the Labradors, and King of the Canines. And nearly fourteen years later, near the end of this story, my determined efforts to drive Simba from one end of the country to the other—so he could see Laureen and the girls one more time before he died—would seem less like an act of mercy and more like a matter of respect—and by that point, love.

2. COURTING THE DOG

San Francisco, California
October 2003

I met Laureen at a snazzy San Francisco watering hole called the Redwood Room three years after Simba joined her household but only hours after the Fulton County Court finalized her divorce from Guenter. A volatile brew of alcohol, late nights, and star-struck young women eventually propels nearly every celebrity chef toward the cheatin' side of town. And as Laureen always said, Guenter wasn't built for fidelity. So after eleven years of marriage and a remarkable fourteen-year run as an undefeated trial lawyer, forty-two-year-old Laureen found herself a single working mother of two small girls and one very large dog.

With fifty-something Guenter off playing house with a waitress-slash-ballerina less than half his age, Laureen resolved to spend more time at home with Angela and Grace. And since in-house lawyers keep far shorter, more regular hours than trial lawyers, she reluctantly quit the courtroom she loved and took a new position—as head lawyer of the technology division of a mammoth health-care conglomerate called the McKesson Corporation. McKesson's tech operations were based in Atlanta, where Laureen lived. But its parent company was headquartered in a thirty-seven-story office tower in downtown San Francisco, which was my hometown.

When McKesson's worldwide law department meeting wound to a close on October 23, 2003, four of Laureen's colleagues—three men and a woman—informed her in no uncertain terms that they were taking her out on the town. The purpose of the mission, the lawyers half-joked, was to celebrate Laureen's brand-new officially single status and to scout some fresh romantic prospects. So when the PowerPoints faded and the laptops snapped shut, the four pushy lawyers grabbed up Laureen and dragged her across San Francisco's Union Square to the Redwood Room in the hip Clift Hotel.

By coincidence, I was also at the Redwood Room that evening. At forty-eight, I was bravely enduring my own immensely crappy divorce. And I had three school-age children—sixteen-year-old Kara, fourteen-year-old Willie, and nine-year-old Lucas. So generally speaking, you wouldn't have found me whiling away a crisp autumn eve at some ritzy downtown nightspot. But that particular crisp autumn eve my New York editor was in town to help me celebrate my new book's debut on the *New York Times* bestseller list (after, it must be said, a prolonged bestseller drought).

When our self-congratulatory wine-soaked dinner wound to a close, I realized I needed some air. So I offered to walk the editor back to his hotel. He said he was staying at the Clift, which was only twelve blocks away, so off we went.

When we hit the Clift's lobby, the festive din emanating from the Redwood Room matched our high spirits, so we decided to drop in for a nightcap. As I pushed my way into the cavernous redwood-paneled bar packed with what must have been two hundred or more significantly younger revelers, I had no idea that I was about to become the target of a romantic manhunt mounted by a team of corporate lawyers. All I knew was that my bad back was kicking up. And I desperately wanted to plunk myself down in a chair somewhere so I could nurse my L4 vertebra and a Grey Goose martini. But it was a Friday night. The joint was jumpin'. And it looked like standing room only.

Within a matter of minutes, I lost sight of my tipsy publishing colleague, who had likely retreated to his room. So I bemoaned by plight instead to a well-tailored young woman who was loitering at the jammed art deco bar tapping her Jimmy Choos to the house music. Her name was Ami Patel. And she turned out to be one of the intrepid McKesson attorneys who were hard on the hunt for Laureen's new mate.

After a quick glance at my ring finger, the wily Ms. Patel posed a few deceptively casual questions about my age, occupation, and marital status. And then, sensing prey, she deftly steered me toward a burgundy velvet settee where Laureen—slim, blonde, and elegant—was already in the process of being wooed by another suitor, a gawky six-foot-five anesthesiologist who was up from LA for some sort of medical convention.

I subsequently learned that the McKesson lawyers had also recruited the towering anesthesiologist, whom they dubbed Bachelor Number One. Which of course made me Bachelor Number Two— doomed to languish in the bull pen until the starter lost his mojo.

But since I was still oblivious to any of this nonsense, I was just grateful for the seat and content to sip my ice-cold martini while smugly eavesdropping on the good doctor's tortured mating patter.

For better or worse, Laureen has always skewed toward impetuous creative types—like chefs and authors—so when the monotonous MD took a bathroom break, she finally turned her attention my way. I decided to open with a joke. So I asked her if the anesthesiologist was putting her to sleep. Admittedly weak, but Laureen was kind enough to chuckle. So we bantered back and forth for maybe twenty minutes. And during that brief interval, I'm reliably informed (by Laureen) that I blustered on shamelessly about my new bestseller and issued an impromptu invitation to its upcoming launch party at the New York Public Library—a brash solicitation she prudently declined. When our conversation ran its natural course and I realized, perhaps too late, that vodka poured on top of red wine might actually be rendering me less, rather than more, debonair, I bid Laureen adieu. We routinely exchanged business cards—hers very corporate, mine recently printed at Kinko's—and that, I figured, was that.

Laureen was a stunner—five foot nine, with an enormous smile and a quietly confident demeanor. But she lived clear on the other side of the country, in Georgia of all places, where she apparently had a proper corporate job, two pretty little girls, and a big crazy dog. I was bound to San Francisco, a city I loved, not by my work—I could do that anywhere—but by three school-age children and a sporadically belligerent ex-wife with whom I shared custody on a fifty-fifty basis. Laureen didn't seem like a casual relationship kind of gal. So what would be the point?

Anyway that was the logic of it. But as we all learn at some point in our lives, logic has its limits. And about two months after our fleeting barroom encounter, I received a "remember me?" email from Laureen. She wrote that she was returning to San Francisco for the company Christmas party. She also said I looked a bit like Ryan O'Neal. And she wondered whether I might like to have a drink with her.

Of course, I remembered her. And I sincerely hoped she meant the handsome *Love Story*-era Ryan O'Neal and not the puffy, old man-boob Ryan O'Neal who occasionally turned up in "Where Are They Now?" photos—although I knew the latter was probably closer to the mark. But, yes, either way, I did want to reconnect. So I threw all prudent geographical considerations to the wind and invited Laureen to meet me at the very same bench in the Redwood Room—which seemed, to me at least, to be a vaguely romantic gesture.

On the appointed evening, I found myself getting all dressed up in a blue blazer, gray slacks and a powder blue shirt, all courtesy of the Brooks Brothers factory outlet in Petaluma. I arrived an hour early so I could secure the seats in question. And when Laureen wafted in wearing a starched white blouse with French cuffs and silver cufflinks, a charcoal pencil skirt, and some pretty pricey-looking riding boots, she was just as engaging and sophisticated as I remembered through my wine-and-vodka haze. Laureen flashed her megawatt smile. Sparks flew. And that very evening we initiated a long-distance romance that would culminate at the altar two years later—all thanks to four very pushy lawyers who tried to play Cupid and, oddly enough, succeeded.

During our two-year courtship, Laureen visited San Francisco every other month, and on alternating months, I traveled to Atlanta—usually for a weekend, but sometimes for as long as a week. At that point, Simba was three years old and at the peak of his impressive physical prowess. I wasn't around for his wayward puppy years, but by all accounts, Simba was a holy terror.

Laureen—Lolly to her family and childhood friends—grew up the youngest of ten children in a ridiculously small (given the number of occupants) red brick house in a pleasant residential section of Milwaukee called Whitefish Bay. There—as if ten children weren't enough—her staunchly Catholic parents bred Boston terriers and bichon frises to make a little scratch on the side. As a consequence, Laureen was intimately familiar with the care and training of puppies and had every reason to believe that she could tackle even a hard case like Simba. Early on, when Laureen still harbored that illusion, she signed Simba up for a standard six-week puppy-training course at her local pet store in Atlanta. The program's goals were modest. Puppies would learn the basic commands—sit, stay, lie down, and come. They would be taught to parade around on their leashes, and if all went well, to amicably commingle with other members of their species.

Simba refused to do any one of those things. During his very first training session, he leapt up on every other dog and human in the room. He ignored Laureen's commands. He repeatedly crashed through the low plastic fence that defined the training area. And he made it clear that he regarded his leash a grave personal insult. At the end of the first two-hour session, Simba was branded a delinquent and summarily expelled from the group.

"I think it would be better for the other dogs," said the young female trainer in khaki shorts and a polo shirt.

Laureen took a deep breath, looked the trainer straight in the eye, and employed her most persuasive trial-lawyer tone—which, believe me, is pretty persuasive.

"I understand this evening's session didn't go particularly well," Laureen said very calmly, like she was addressing a jury. "But if you would be kind enough to give us one more opportunity, I'm confident that we can do better next week. Can you give us that opportunity?"

"Yeah, I'd like to help you with that," the young trainer replied. "But you saw what happened here tonight. It was chaos. I've been teaching the puppy class for more than a year, and I've never seen anything like it. I'm pretty sure we won't be able to do anything with *that* dog." Then she pointed at little Simba in a very "*J'accuse!*" sort of way, and he gazed up at her and smiled.

"If I were you," she continued, "I would look into private lessons. Or better yet, give that dog back to whoever sold him to you." And with that, she turned on her heel and walked briskly toward the break room.

"It's my ex-husband's fault," Laureen cried out after her. "He brought home the wrong dog!"

But by then, of course, it was too late.

Laureen, who is accustomed to across-the-board success in all of her endeavors, was humiliated but undaunted. She swooped into her trademark research mode and quickly turned up a no-nonsense "canine behavior consultant" who lived in Brooklyn. Despite the ridiculous expense, Laureen flew the tough New Yorker down to Atlanta. And in less than two weeks, she transformed Simba from a feral little brute into something roughly approximating a family pet. I don't know exactly what the trainer did or how she did it. But it was such a traumatic experience for baby Simba that years later if Laureen barked orders at him in a Brooklyn accent ("Go-wahn, Simba, go-wahn,") he would immediately recall his boot-camp days, shudder, and meekly comply.

The first time I visited Laureen in Atlanta, I knew that if I truly wanted a future with her, I would have to win the hearts of both her daughters and her dog. Because, as anyone who's ever tried it will tell you, when you date a single mom, you pretty much date her entire family.

Grace, who was four at the time, was the easiest nut to crack. When her mother told her I was coming for a visit, Grace misheard my name and thought it was Chen—the same as an Asian girl at her nursery school. So, naturally, she expected me to be Chinese—a prospect that seemed to please her immensely. When she first clapped eyes on my plainly Caucasian features, she was visibly disappointed. But within a matter of days, I was able to win her over with a few of the classics—piggyback rides, the tickle monster, candy, and a stupid song I made up about frozen polar bear poop.

At six, Angela was so shy that she literally shook with fear whenever she was compelled to attend a classmate's birthday party. So it took us a bit longer to forge a connection. Fortunately, she didn't expect me to be Chinese. But when her father ran off with his lanky young paramour, Angela zeroed in on a very specific replacement—namely Atlanta Falcons starting quarterback Michael Vick. Angela, who was every inch a tomboy at the time, thought Vick might be better than her original German-born, soccer-raised father when it came to tossing a ball around the backyard—which was probably a fair assumption.

It took awhile for Angela to relinquish her NFL dreams, but I can throw a ball as well as the next native-born American. And four years later, when Michael Vick was sentenced to twenty-three months in Leavenworth for operating a vicious dog-fighting ring, I looked pretty good by comparison. Angela also thought for some reason that Dr. Martin Luther King was a leprechaun. But I decided not to disabuse her of that particular historical inaccuracy, at least for the time being.

Simba was a whole other story. In my admittedly limited experience, Labradors—even proud Labradors like Simba—can be seduced in four ways:

1. Feed them.
2. Throw them a ball.
3. Take them for walks.
4. Scratch their tummies.

Dispensing treats all day would have been the quickest, most efficacious way to go. Labs, after all, are all about the grub. But in the long run, it wouldn't have been the healthiest regime. This was subsequently proven by Angela and Grace's Brazilian au pair, Andrea. During her otherwise very pleasant year with us, Andrea tried to win Simba's heart and mind through his stomach. And by the time Laureen discovered her nefarious scheme, she'd managed to plump Simba up into a happy, lazy, 110-pound couch potato.

Laureen would have come down harder on Andrea, but honestly, she had already punished herself. Because as Andrea massively overfed the dog, she, like a surprisingly large number of foreign au pairs, became enamored with the caloric wonders of a chain restaurant called the Cheesecake Factory. And in a stroke of karmic justice, the Cheesecake Factory did to her exactly what she did to Simba, piling twenty-five pounds onto her previously slender frame. Happily, when Andrea finished her year in America and returned to her native land, both she and the dog resumed their original size and weight.

As for fetching a ball . . . well, Simba simply wouldn't do it. I could never quite wrap my mind around that cold, hard fact. In my mid-thirties and early forties, I had an affable yellow Lab named Ginger who devoted the best years of her life to incessantly dropping a neon green tennis ball at my feet. Whenever I relented and took her out to the backyard, she would retrieve the ball a hundred times in a row with no visible decrease in enthusiasm. I'm convinced that if I'd thrown the ball for three hours straight, Ginger—who wasn't exactly the Einstein of Labradors—would have cheerfully returned it over and over again until she dropped dead from exhaustion, an ecstatic smile plastered across her guileless face.

But whenever I took Simba outside, threw a tennis ball across the lawn, and bellowed, "Get it, Simba! Get it!"—even in a Brooklyn accent—he would just sit there and look at me in his bemused patrician way as if to say, "And what would be the point of *that*?"

And I would patiently explain to him that this is what Labradors are meant to do. "For more than two hundred years," I told him, "your ancestors have been bred as hunting dogs. That means when I shoot a duck, you joyously leap into the pond and bring it to me. Well, luckily for you, I don't hunt ducks, and we don't have a pond. But when I throw a tennis ball—which, in this case, is a proxy for the duck—you are compelled by two full centuries of breeding to fetch it. It's in your blood, Simba. In fact, the full name of your breed is Labrador *retriever*, not Labrador "Just-sit-there-and-look-at-me-when-I-throw-a-ball."

But Simba, who was trained by a New York dog whisperer, not a Georgia duck hunter, had no interest whatsoever. And he was smart and proud enough to know that all of that running back and forth signified nothing and hardly befit his august stature.

So in terms of winning Simba over, that left affectionate scratching and long walks. The scratching was no problem. Simba was only too happy to roll right over and receive his due. He would lie on his back, curl up his front legs, and loll his head back with an appallingly goofy look on his enormous face. With his big brown eyes bulging and his long pink tongue hanging out from the side of his mouth, it was one of the few circumstances when he didn't look the least bit noble.

Walking Simba was a much bigger challenge. The tip-off came the first time I approached Laureen's front door in Atlanta. As I climbed the steps of the red brick townhouse where Laureen moved after her divorce, Simba barked with immense enthusiasm. Clearly, whatever qualities he lacked as a gun dog, he more than made up for them as a watchdog. From the first day Simba joined her household, Laureen no longer needed an alarm system or even a doorbell. Because whenever an unsuspecting citizen mounted her steps, pulled into her driveway, or even casually strolled past her house on a sultry Georgia eve, Simba would sound the alarm with gusto.

But to be clear, Simba was a watchdog, not a guard dog. He was still a Labrador after all. And Labradors, with few exceptions, are far more bark than bite. In fact, Simba often found himself fiercely woofing at his front end while cordially wagging in the rear. He seemed unbothered by the contradiction, and any intruder who ignored his ruckus would have had very little to fear.

So despite his big show of protective clamor as I mounted Laureen's steps, when I actually got inside, Simba didn't growl, jump up, or bare his fangs. Instead, he inexplicably turned tail and sprinted full speed down a long hallway toward the rear of the house. Then he rounded the kitchen island, zoomed back through the dining room and across the living room to his starting point. Adults and small children alike pressed their backs to the wall in alarm as ninety pounds of galloping Labrador barreled by.

"Is there something wrong with him?" I asked Laureen.

Laureen shrugged and said, "I don't know. Maybe. It's just what he does. He gets overexcited when new people come to the house. And I guess all that running around calms him down. But don't worry. Once he does a few laps, he'll be fine."

And that turned out to be true. After sprinting his indoor loop three times in succession, Simba was sufficiently composed to greet me, which he then did quite nicely.

So if that was how Simba said hello, what would he do when we sallied forth together into the great outdoors?

In the late eighteenth and early nineteenth centuries, when people still lit their homes with whale oil lamps, Nantucket Island, off the coast of Cape Cod, was the hub of America's energy industry. That's because stout Nantucket whalers were intrepid enough to set forth in twenty-foot open boats, harpoon giant sperm whales, and then hang on for dear life as the leviathans made a run for it. This was called a "Nantucket sleigh ride," and it was sort of what it was like to walk Simba. From the moment we stepped through the front door, Simba strained his leather leash to the breaking point. And I just held on as best I could.

The Nantucket whalers would have to keep their harpoon lines taut until the whale exhausted itself. But I only had to maintain my grip on Simba's leash until he stopped to poop—precisely three times per walk—or pee—every few hundred yards since Simba dispensed his urine judiciously in order to mark as much territory as possible.

As you might guess, Laureen was far more disciplined about all of this than I was. When Laureen walked Simba, she shortened his leash, yanked hard on his choke collar, and yelled, "Heel, Simba, heel!" every few steps until the dog more or less submitted to her will—usually less. My goal, however, was not to train Simba but to win his affection. So I left that particular aspect of Simba's pedagogy to Laureen, and I only reined in the galloping Labrador when we encountered other dogs—confrontations that occasionally turned contentious.

Despite his alpha disposition, or perhaps because of it, Simba almost never barked or growled at his fellow canines. But a surprisingly large number of dogs—almost always much smaller dogs—felt the compulsion to bark and growl at him. Simba generally brushed off these *poseurs* with haughty disdain. But every so often, he sensed a genuine threat. Then, as he silently assumed his defensive posture, his hackles rose and his big brown eyes went flat and steely cold.

The way I saw it, Simba was an old-fashioned "Greatest Generation" sort of dog. He practiced what my father, a former Eighty-second Airborne paratrooper, preached. Namely, that you should never start a fight, but you always finish it. In fact, the one time Simba was physically attacked—by a pair of ridiculous off-leash Pomeranians on a California nature trail—he acquitted himself with conspicuous valor, wounding one Pomeranian in the haunch but stopping well short of the canicide of which he was clearly capable.

Simba's inclination to use only the minimum necessary violence was confirmed years later when Laureen's best friend Tamera brought her handsome, six-month-old, cinnamon-colored vizsla over for a visit. Simba had recently returned from a walk and just wanted to lie down in peace. But young Mikos, full of beans, kept yapping in his face, trying to get Simba to play with him. After several minutes of that nonsense, Simba slowly rose to his feet and shook himself briefly. And then, with neither bark nor growl, he simply took Mikos's entire head into his enormous mouth.

Simba didn't chomp down on Mikos's skull or hurt him in any way. He just wanted to let the young whippersnapper know that he was the boss. And if pushed too far, the boss could literally bite his head off. This had the desired effect. Mikos skulked away whimpering with his tail between his legs and spent the next several hours tucked safely between his owner's knees. Simba, point made, resumed his siesta.

Anyway, whenever I traveled to Atlanta to visit Laureen and the girls, I tried to walk Simba as often as possible. Every evening after dinner, I scratched his belly. And during the course of the day, I dispensed treats sparingly. (Laureen might take issue with that.) In time, Simba accepted me as a member of his pack and eventually as his alpha. He stopped barking maniacally when I climbed Laureen's steps. And he no longer broke into his frenzied hundred-yard dash when I stepped inside. Despite all that—and despite the fact that Simba would eventually become my most constant companion for nearly a decade—he never, ever, even once, fetched a ball for me.

3. STEPDOG

Two years into our long-distance romance, I bought an engagement ring and filled my bedroom with twenty candles of various heights. Then I waited forty minutes for Laureen to get off an evening conference call, dropped to one knee, and proposed marriage. Now we could no longer delay the inevitable. One of us would have to move.

Laureen had a perfectly good job in Atlanta. But after six years as a divisional general counsel she was pretty bored with the work. We figured her digital law experience might land her a more interesting, better-paying job in the Bay Area's booming tech sector. And more to the point, the terms of Laureen's divorce settlement granted her sole custody of Angela, Grace, and Simba. So Guenter the Chef couldn't prevent her from leaving Atlanta even if he wanted to—which, it turned out, he didn't.

There was no way my ex-wife would have had the same laissez-faire attitude. And I knew my California kids would never move to Atlanta. So given all that, Laureen agreed to relocate to San Francisco where we would merge our families.

At the time, I told Laureen how much I appreciated the fact that she was willing to leave a city she loved full of friends she adored to marry the likes of me. And to assuage my guilt, I handed her a chit she could redeem somewhere down the road.

"This time, you're coming to San Francisco to be with me," I told her, "and you know I'm grateful for that. But I know you, Laureen. You're smart and ambitious. And someday you're going to want to take a bigger, better job in some other city. So here's my promise. Once Lucas heads off to college, which is only six years from now, you can move anywhere you want. And I will follow without complaint."

"I appreciate that," said Laureen. "But for now, why don't we just focus on finding me a job in San Francisco and a house big enough for seven people. You know how deep-rooted I am. I moved to Atlanta right after law school, and I stayed there for more than twenty years. I'd still be living there if you hadn't come along. So we'll probably end up living in San Francisco for the rest of our lives."

The moment Laureen said that, I had a strong premonition we'd be moving someday. But all I said was, "Well, that would be great, but remember: the offer stands."

Although I did chauffeur Laureen to a few random job interviews—like the general counsel position at brand new Virgin America Airlines—it turned out to be unnecessary. Because in a stroke of great timing, McKesson's own general counsel—the company's top lawyer and Laureen's boss's boss—suddenly decided to retire after more than two decades at the helm. And while Laureen no longer wanted to head up a divisional law department—the equivalent of middle management—McKesson's top legal job, based in San Francisco and far more prestigious—appealed to her striving nature.

Laureen and I had long discussions about whether she should pursue the position. The $300 billion drug distribution business has always been a boys' club—even more so than other industries. And in the storied 173-year history of the McKesson Corporation, no woman had ever been chief legal officer or chief anything officer for that matter. And even if you put gender aside, Laureen objectively lacked the deep securities experience normally required to be head lawyer of a large, publicly traded company.

There would also be some unpleasantness involved. To prevail, Laureen would have to leapfrog her own boss, McKesson's longtime deputy general counsel, who, with a certain degree of justification, considered the top job his hard-earned due. He would view any expression of interest on Laureen's part as rank insubordination. And whoever lost that battle would likely have to pack up their files and set sail for another company.

Despite all that—and despite the fact that McKesson mounted a formal nationwide search—Laureen threw her hat in the ring, arguing that what the company really needed was a rock-solid manager and battle-tested trial lawyer—for the times when McKesson, like all large corporations, faced existential legal conflict. As for securities law, Laureen assured her CEO that she could hire a specialist to handle that aspect of the job while she got up to speed.

Laureen must have been persuasive, because after a months-long vetting process, the company's dynamic young CEO—a fellow Midwesterner from Minnesota—decided to give her the shot. Suddenly Laureen was no longer a mid-level corporate lawyer. She was now executive vice president, general counsel, and corporate secretary of America's fourteenth largest corporation by sales. And she headed up an international law department that employed nearly 400 attorneys, paralegals, and assistants. McKesson wasn't a household name like General Electric or Wells Fargo, but it was a hundred-billion-dollar-a-year enterprise in a tightly regulated industry. So for a lawyer, this was the big time.

In May 2006, Laureen and I bought a house roomy enough for five kids and a dog. It was your typical Bay Area craftsman home with brown shingles and hunter-green trim set on a quiet wooded acre eight miles north of the Golden Gate Bridge in scenic Marin County. I prepared the house for our newly merged family while Laureen frantically flew back and forth across the country, trying to do her old job in Atlanta and her new job in San Francisco at the same time. In June, Laureen, Angela, Grace, and Simba bid Atlanta a teary farewell and joined Kara, Willie, Lucas, and me in our new home.

It was Simba's first, and as it turned out last, airplane ride. And he was not amused. Simba was ensconced as comfortably as possible with his chew toys and bed in what must have been the largest dog crate ever manufactured. And he was mildly sedated for the four-and-a-half-hour flight. Still, it seemed somehow disrespectful to incarcerate the King of the Canines in a big plastic box and shove him into the luggage compartment of an airplane.

When Simba was finally discharged into the baggage claim area of the San Jose airport[1] he was a bit groggy and suitably annoyed. And in his drug-addled state, he nipped Grace's finger when she tried to hug him around the neck. It was a minor injury to be sure. But to Grace, who used to ride around the house on Simba's back, it was an astonishing betrayal. We forgave Simba his bad temper and eventually convinced Grace to do the same. And we figured Simba would forgive us too when he saw his big, new yard, lushly inhabited by deer, raccoons, and wild turkeys that he could chase to his heart's content but never quite catch.

At this point, Kara was about to graduate from high school. Will was a high school junior; Lucas, a sixth-grader; Angela, a second-grader; and Grace, a kindergartener. Our blended family was blessed in many ways. Thanks to Laureen's fancy new job, we could actually afford the big house we just bought. My kids adored Laureen. Hers were willing to give me a chance. And most importantly, all five kids got along well with each other right from the get-go. In fact, they got along a little too well. The five of them promptly formed an ironclad alliance against their common enemy, Laureen and me. And when either of us tried to discipline one child, the other four would vigorously rally to the miscreant's defense with outspoken Angela invariably bearing their standard.

On August 19, 2006, Laureen and I were married at an old stone winery in nearby Napa Valley. The wedding got off to a rocky

---

[1] Laureen didn't fully understand Bay Area geography yet—specifically that Mineta San Jose Airport was an hour and a half from our house as opposed to SFO, which was only thirty minutes away.

start. During the previous year, my seventy-six-year-old mother, who lived in Pittsburgh, Pennsylvania, had become progressively less steady on her feet. In fairly quick progression, she had dislocated her shoulder in one fall and cracked a vertebra in another. But like her mother before her, she stubbornly refused to use either a wheelchair or a walker—only a cane. So as she shuffled up the uneven flagstone path that led from the parking lot to the outdoor wedding site, she tripped and fell flat on her face.

Although the spill was initially dramatic—my mother has never suffered quietly—two of Laureen's many brothers helped her to her feet and cleaned her wounds with a handful of wet paper towels they grabbed from the men's room. Then my sainted father, Norm, rushed over and attempted to calm her down. Twenty minutes later, she hobbled into the ceremony with only a few conspicuous scrapes on her nose and chin. And for the remainder of the happy day, she basked in the solicitous attention of the other wedding guests.

At roughly the same time, Angela—stunning in her black and white bridesmaid's dress—was struck with a serious bout of stage fright and flatly refused to participate in the ceremony. It took Laureen a full thirty minutes to convince Angela—who sat crying on the floor of a hotel closet—that it was her categorical duty to stand up with her younger sister and three new stepsiblings. Eventually she acquiesced. And although the ceremony was delayed, she performed flawlessly in the end.

While we certainly discussed it, we weren't quite crazy enough to march Simba down the aisle with the rest of the wedding party. Somehow that seemed to cross the fine line between dog lover and lunatic. But he did watch majestically from the sidelines, a white bow tied to his leather collar, as a grumpy rabbi and a charismatic defrocked Irish Catholic priest took turns pronouncing us man and wife. When the ceremony concluded with a smattering of applause from Laureen's side of the aisle and a few shouts of "*L'chaim*" from mine, Simba was officially my stepdog.

As you might imagine, five children and a very large dog make for a boisterous household. But it was a happy home, and Simba was no small part of that. I loved watching the kids come home from school each day, one after the other, and break into big smiles when they saw Simba faithfully waiting for them by the front door. Simba greeted each child as a long-lost pack member. But he was practically ecstatic when Laureen came home from work, usually around seven thirty. When Simba heard the garage door rumble open, he leapt up from his customary spot on the brown family-room rug and ran to the top of the stairs that led down to the garage. There he waited, tail madly flailing, until Laureen emerged from the basement. Then he gazed upon her with an unsullied love, buried his enormous head between her knees like a giant Labrador baby, and gratefully received her ministrations.

One secret of Laureen's success is that she has always dressed the part of the chic corporate executive. You'd be shocked at the difference this makes for women approaching the top rung of corporate America. (For men, it hardly matters.) But haute couture wasn't always easy with Simba around. On days when Laureen wore a black skirt or charcoal slacks, Simba would inevitably rub up against her mere seconds before she left for work, instantly blanketing her smart ensemble with hundreds of short, white dog hairs. In fact, all of our clothes and most of our furniture were perpetually upholstered in Labrador fur. And when Simba rode in the car with us, the air vents would kick up visible cyclones of dog hair that eventually settled like fresh snow on everyone in the vehicle.

But that was a small price to pay for Simba's companionship. Because in this much too serious world, dogs give us license to act foolishly. Since I have that propensity anyway, I took full advantage of the situation. But, believe me, I wasn't the only one who did that. Grace set up a Facebook page where she faithfully reported Simba's noteworthy activities to his twenty-four "friends." Every Halloween Lucas dressed him up in costumes that inevitably involved Ray-Bans and a fedora. And every few months or so, Angela painted his black toenails pink, blue, or both.

When Willie pissed off his younger siblings (which happened fairly regularly), they would often sneak into his room, swipe a pair of his boxer shorts, and let Simba wear them around the house for a while before carefully replacing them in his drawer. Even Laureen would return from the C-suite where she defended billion-dollar lawsuits all day, plunk herself down on the rug next to Simba, and regale him with goofy baby talk.

But like I said, I was the ringleader. I taught Simba tricks that insulted his innate nobility. I taught him to catch little biscuits in his mouth from ten feet across the kitchen. And when I sang, "Who likes to dance? Who likes to dance?" Simba, trained with dog treats, would jump up and place his front paws on my shoulders. Then we would twirl around the kitchen for a while. And probably because I was raised on sixties cartoons and sitcoms, I composed a stupid theme song for Simba that the kids sang all the time and Kara once scored in three-part harmony.

I had time for these shenanigans because Simba and I spent nearly all day every day together. As I worked in my home office writing and designing coffee-table books for Barnes & Noble, Simba was my shadow. When I sat at my desk, Simba lay next to me. When I stood up, he stood up. When I ambled over to the kitchen to make a sandwich or cook dinner, Simba hovered underfoot waiting for a morsel of food to drop (which sometimes happened accidently and sometimes accidently on purpose.)

Simba and I learned to communicate with a fairly extensive vocabulary of words and gestures. If I held my hand parallel to the floor, Simba sat. If I wordlessly pointed to the ground, he lay down. If I opened the back door and said, "Go on, Simba," he ran outside and peed. If I said, "Hey, Simba, wanna go for a ride?" he sprinted out the front door and stood next to my car panting with anticipation. And if I opened the front closet where we hung his leash, he suddenly became the happiest dog on Earth.

Over time, Laureen broke Simba of his maniacal watchdog tendencies. And eventually, whenever somebody yelled, "Simba, go to your spot!" he would reluctantly stop woofing at whoever dared to darken our door and would run instead to a little first floor powder room where he sat quietly on the rug until someone released him. In Simba's mind, this relieved him of his sacred duty to defend the homeland. And only by way of penance will I tell you that we sometimes forgot where he was until someone had to use the toilet or someone else said, "Hey, where's Simba?"

But the conversation wasn't one-way. As I trained Simba, he trained me. When he wanted me to go somewhere or do something, he approached me, looked me straight in the eye, and backed up a few steps. That meant, "Come with me." Then he would lead me to the back door if he needed to pee, or to his water bowl if he wanted me to refill it, or up to Angela's room if he wanted to retire for the evening. (There were some bedtime formalities that required my participation.) If Simba wanted his tummy rubbed, he would lead me to the family room rug, roll over, and give me one of his inelegant "scratch-me" looks.

Simba, no longer the *enfant terrible*, was now unfailingly courteous about all of this. He rarely interrupted me while I worked at my desk or even as I lay on the couch watching TV. He would just wait patiently until I stood up, and then he would respectfully submit his request. If he ever broke that protocol, I knew it meant he really had to pee or that wild animals—usually deer, turkeys, or raccoons—had invaded our yard.

One of Simba's most endearing gestures was pure love. After dinner each evening, I would make my way from the kitchen table to the rug in front of the fireplace and lie down next to Simba—just to let him know that he remained, as always, a cherished member of the pack. Then Simba, in what seemed to be a very human or perhaps just a universal act of affection, would lay one of his huge, white paws on top of my arm as if to comfort me—or maybe just to make a physical connection.

Of course, we never know precisely what dogs are thinking. But if this was Simba's way of saying of saying "I love you," then the feeling was entirely mutual. For none of us could imagine the life of our family without him.

4. OLD DOG

In absolute terms, the time that passed from Simba's arrival on the West Coast until his first serious health crisis was only seven years. But in dog years, it was more like half a century. With dogs you see the human life cycle in condensed form. Simba was a terrible toddler for six months, a wild child for a year, and a rambunctious teenager for a year and a half. He was a strutting young adult for three years, and then a middle-aged gentleman for five or six years after that. But by April 2013, at twelve-and-a-half years of age, Simba could only be described as an old dog—the human equivalent of eighty-five or ninety. Most Labrador retrievers never see their thirteenth birthday. The breed's median lifespan is just over eleven years. But Laureen desperately wanted to believe that Simba's immense strength and stamina would sustain him well past the average. In fact we were all convinced that Simba would be a special case.

For both dogs and people, old age is the slow and relentless stripping away of the things we love. And there was nothing Simba loved more than long walks—particularly his weekend constitutionals with Laureen in Blackie's Pasture on the grassy shores of Richardson Bay. There, Simba enjoyed the magnificent scenery that stretched from Mt. Tamalpais to the Golden Gate Bridge. And he would regally meet and greet other neighborhood dogs. During these weekend promenades, Laureen would often chat with her fellow dog enthusiasts who invariably commented on Simba's imposing size, handsome countenance, and aristocratic bearing.

"Is that a yellow Lab?" they would ask. "He's huge."

And Laureen, ever the proud mother, would tell the inquirer that Simba was the biggest puppy in his litter (this bug had evolved into a feature over the years), that his ancestors were dog show champions, and that Simba was, in fact, not a yellow Lab, but a white Lab with honey-dipped ears. Laureen always topped off the conversation by casually mentioning how old Simba was.

"Wow, he looks great for his age," they inevitably replied—and he did.

Although Simba's walks with Laureen persisted well into his dotage, at twelve and a half, Simba no longer strained the leash like some sort of satanic sled dog. Now he gently strolled beside Laureen like the polite old pensioner he'd become—like Laureen had tried to teach him years ago, but which Simba couldn't quite manage until his life force had sufficiently ebbed.

In his prime, Simba could easily trot seven or eight miles at a clip—and in that regard, fit, outdoorsy Laureen was the perfect companion. But now if Simba walked more than a mile or two, even at a measured pace, his arthritis would flare up. And for the rest of the day, he would lie nearly motionless on his side. When

Simba did finally stand up, it was always very slowly and with visibly painful effort. Then he pitifully limped around the kitchen for a while until we gave him an extra dose of his liver-flavored anti-inflammatory tablets.

We also no longer had to worry about Simba humping other dogs—males to assert his dominance, females out of sheer lust. Despite the fact he was neutered as a puppy—an admittedly barbaric act that was supposed to forefend that sort of behavior—we often had to step in and yank Simba off other dogs. And once, after Laureen and I managed to pry him loose from a particularly beguiling, coffee-colored French Poodle in the parking lot of Lucas's high school, he remained hunched over, back arched and fully aroused, dramatically humping the air.

"Oh, no. Can you do something about that?" asked Laureen, who was truly horrified by the untoward spectacle of her dog simulating a sex act in front of Lucas's school.

"What do you suggest?" I replied.

"There's a water bottle in the car. Can you just get it and pour some water on his head?"

"You mean like a cold shower?" I asked.

"Yes, like a cold shower. Please, David. Just do it."

"No, I don't think so," I replied. "That would just make us look even more ridiculous—if that's even possible. We should probably just let it run its course."

Which it eventually did, but not before a small crowd of parents and children, waiting for the school bus to return from a field trip, were variously amused and horrified by Simba's prurient display.

But now, in his golden years, Simba barely gave the ladies a second look. And when the FedEx guy or the gardeners came to the house, he no longer went berserk. In fact, more often than not, he didn't bother to get up at all. He just lay on the rug and let loose a few half-hearted woofs to let us know that he still understood his duty but now lacked the stamina to execute it.

There was, however, one magical place where Simba regained a measure of his youthful vigor. In February 2011, Laureen bought a vacation home on California's rocky Sonoma Coast. I initially told Laureen that I had no interest whatsoever in owning a second home with all of its attendant expense and time-consuming maintenance.

"For a lot less money," I argued, "we can take vacations wherever we want."

But since her promotion to general counsel of McKesson, Laureen lived—or at least worked—in a world where all of her colleagues owned, in addition to their so-called "primary residence," a timbered ski chalet in Telluride or a charming Napa Valley farmhouse with a few acres of chardonnay.

Laureen's mother, Jane, died from breast cancer when Laureen was nine years old. And for several years thereafter, her previously successful and charismatic father devolved into an abusive alcoholic with a factory job. With ten kids in the house, money was always tight. So Laureen, the youngest of the brood, grew up sharing a tiny attic bedroom with two older sisters and wearing their hand-me-down clothes. When her father told her that there was no good reason for her to go to college "because she could always get a good job as a secretary," Laureen finished high school in three years and then worked full time for a year so she could pay her own way through the University of Wisconsin at Eau Claire. There she became an all-American track star, graduated near the top of her class, and was admitted to the University of Wisconsin Law School in Madison.

During law school, Laureen met her educational expenses by assisting professors, cleaning houses, babysitting, and when straits were particularly dire, by selling her own blood. She didn't have any health insurance, so when she shattered her elbow in a bicycle accident, she quickly blew through her meager savings and nearly had to abandon her lifelong dream of becoming a lawyer. Only the compassionate intercession of the University of Wisconsin chancellor, Donna Shalala, rescued her prospective career.

So to the manor Laureen clearly was not born. And the notion of purchasing a vacation home we might use three or four weeks a year would have been as unthinkable to her parents as buying a private jet or a chateau in France. But up on the thirty-seventh floor of the McKesson Building where the top executives worked, owning only one home was considered vaguely aberrant. And in the upper echelons of corporate America, aberrant is something you definitely don't want to be.

Following our initial conversation, I didn't hear anything more on the subject for several months. I took that as good sign and thought maybe the impulse had passed. But true to form, Laureen had been quietly devoting some of her early hours—she got up at four every morning—systematically analyzing every oceanfront listing within a 150-mile radius of our house. She began her search at the south end of the range near tony Carmel-by-the-Sea and systematically worked her way north until she reached a fascinating, if somewhat obscure, eco-community called The Sea Ranch, about 120 miles north of San Francisco.

Designed by a team of visionary, granola-munching, Birkenstock-wearing (I assume) Berkeley architects in the mid-1960s, this former sheep ranch is a narrow ten-mile-long ocean-side strip that combines a very specific architectural sensibility—the starkly simple wooden houses visually melt into the landscape—with a breathtaking coastal setting. It's not a particularly fashionable spot for a second home—like Tahoe or Napa—so Laureen would still have to live with that petty stigma. But Sea Ranch's rocky ocean-sprayed cliffs, pocket-sized beaches, and wildflower-bejeweled meadows simply take your breath away.

There Laureen found a simple, boxy "mineshaft-style" house perched on a thirty-foot cliff above the gray green Pacific breakers. Built by a childless Ohio couple who suffered a financial setback, the house was only five years old and didn't require much in the way of repairs or improvement. Furthermore, the Ohio couple—who from the look of things had far better taste than we did—wanted to sell the house fully furnished right down to the silverware, dishes, and towels. So it wouldn't take us months to set up second house-keeping.

And as usual, Laureen was right. The entire family loved Sea Ranch right from the start. It was a healthful, relaxing place where you could sit in a weathered wooden rocking chair on the back deck, watching spouting gray whales migrate north and south. Or hike along the magnificent oceanside trail that ran behind our house. Or in twenty-two-year-old Will's case, invite young ladies—usually au pairs from the Nordic nations—up for a romantic weekend.

But nobody loved Sea Ranch more than Simba. He clearly didn't relish the windy gut-twisting drive up the stunningly scenic two-lane coastal highway. But the moment we pulled into the driveway and he heard gravel crunching under the tires, he snapped to attention and panted with anticipation.

As good old Simba leapt gingerly from the back of the station wagon, you could practically see the years melt away. He would always pause in the middle of the driveway for a few minutes, holding his massive head perfectly still as he sniffed the salt air and listened to the breakers crashing rhythmically on the bluff behind the house.

Labrador retrievers were originally called St. John's water dogs. And they likely originated on Newfoundland's rugged Avalon Peninsula, which juts into the icy North Atlantic. So Simba's affinity for rocky seashores and brisk ocean breezes may have been some sort of breed memory. But whatever the reason, Sea Ranch always seemed to breathe fresh life into him.

Whenever he was at Sea Ranch, Simba's appetite sharpened. He could walk farther than usual ,and he would even trot thirty or forty yards across the dark wet sand at nearby Walk-on Beach. And each day when he returned from his jaunt, he would lie regally on a three-by-three-foot area rug left behind by the previous owners. The tan wool rug had a series of black numbers woven into it that allegedly represented the precise latitude and longitude of the house. And it was set squarely in the middle of the big central room that served as our combination kitchen-dining-family room. From that strategic post, his acknowledged place in the house, Simba would placidly observe the life of the family as it swirled around him during the course of the day. And sooner or later, one after another, everyone in the family would kneel down before him and pay homage to the Lord of the Labradors, patting his enormous head and telling him what a good dog he was.

Simba even had his own specialized Sea Ranch duty—barking menacingly at the small gray fox that brazenly employed our back deck as his toilet. And even in the autumn of his life, when he could no longer be bothered to menace the gardeners or bark at the mail carrier, Simba gave that particular duty his all. The Sea Ranch, in short, was Simba's Shangri-la. And he was happier there than he was anywhere else on Earth.

But back home in Tiburon, Simba was an increasingly frequent visitor to nearby Tamalpais Pet Hospital. He was plagued by many of the maladies common to old Labradors and other large-breed dogs. First came the lumps. It began with just one or two. Simba's vet, Dr. Penny Elliott, always biopsied them just to be safe, but she assured us that these soft fatty tumors, called lipomas, were almost always benign and that we really shouldn't worry about them. But then, when Simba was ten, one of his lumps, harder than the others, turned out to be malignant. The cancer wasn't life threatening or anything, just an overnight stay at the pet hospital and a surprisingly large medical bill.

Every three months or so for the next two years, Dr. Elliott methodically palpated, measured, and recorded every one of Simba's many lumps—some as large as small lemons—on a blue chart tucked into his burgeoning file. But then, after a while, the lumps became so large and so prolific—and frankly, Simba got so old—that she simply stopped tracking them. It was kind of like when my father developed a slow-growing form of prostate cancer at age seventy-eight. The oncologist told him that, given his advanced age, no action would be taken because, and I quote, "You're going to die, but not from this." That's when you know that the end of the road, while maybe not just around the next bend, is lurking somewhere out there on the horizon.

Despite his lumps and his cancer and his painful arthritis and his waning strength and stamina, I had almost as much trouble as Laureen accepting the fact that Simba was no longer the hardy athletic dog I had known for more than a decade. Sure, he couldn't walk more than a half hour anymore, but he was as enthusiastic as ever when I grabbed his leash off the hook. And while he no longer loped up the front steps like a young gazelle, he could still climb them at a slow trot. And if Simba had ceased barking maniacally at every sentient being who dared to enter his territory, maybe that was a good thing. "Even cancer couldn't kill him," I always said.

But then Simba contracted an unspecified snout infection. And unlike his previous illnesses, he couldn't just shake this one off. The bug, whatever it was, knocked out Simba's sense of smell, which is pretty serious business for a dog. When Simba couldn't smell his food, he lost his appetite. And when I poured the kibble into his big aluminum bowl, instead of wolfing it down like he usually did, he just glanced at it and shuffled away.

The infection also upset Simba's sense of balance and, like my mother, he began to stumble and fall down from time to time. Falls are nature's way of culling the pack. Before humans settled into permanent agricultural communities ten thousand years ago—and dogs followed close behind—both species hunted nomadically. And when old or infirm members of the tribe, or the pack, stumbled and couldn't get up, they were left to die. It seems heartless now, but with its weakest members culled, the group as a whole stood a better chance of survival. So in both Simba's case and my mother's, I regarded their frequent falls as dark harbingers.

When Simba contracted his snout infection and started falling down, we were having some work done at the house. And there were always two or three construction workers on the premises including Randy Hitchcock, my longtime friend and contractor. Early one morning, Simba and I heard Randy's mammoth Ford F-250 pickup rumble up the driveway. And as we sauntered out to greet him, Simba was all excited to see his old buddy Randy. But then Simba's legs suddenly buckled out from under him, and he collapsed in a heap on the pavers.

Simba desperately tried to pull himself up again, but this time he couldn't do it. And as he tried over and over again, his breath shortened, and his eyes widened with panic. I tried to calm him by saying, "C'mon, buddy. It's okay. You can do it. I'll help you."

But even when I straddled Simba and pulled up on his torso, he couldn't regain his footing. And finally Randy had to help me hoist Simba into the backseat of my car so I could rush him to the vet's.

I liked having Randy and his guys around the house. I enjoyed talking to them about joists and trusses and guy stuff like that. I liked it when they needed an extra pair of hands to hold one end of a beam or a window casement or whatever it was they were trying to install. I mean writing and designing coffee-table books is all well and good, but as the revered former picture editor of the *London Sunday Times*, Michael Rand, once said to me, "It's not what you'd call man's work."

So when Randy and his guys were working around the house, I tended to spend more time than usual away from my computer. And I tried—probably with limited success—to be one of the guys. You know, more gritty western Pennsylvania where I was raised, and less snotty Marin County where I ended up. But after Randy and I loaded Simba into the car and the other guys gathered around to see what all the commotion was about, I started saying to Randy, "Hey, thanks man, I appreciate it. I guess I better get him over to the vet's to find out what's going on. Maybe he …"

And at that point, my voice broke, and I began to cry, damn it. I mean I wasn't bawling or anything, but I was clearly crying. And I couldn't have been more embarrassed. Of course I loved Simba. I knew that. But this was nothing to cry about, and certainly not in front of the guys—who by this time were all staring down at their work boots in embarrassment.

I said "Sorry, sorry" a few times. Then I climbed into my car and drove Simba down Tiburon Boulevard and across 101 to Tamalpais Pet Hospital in Mill Valley. I was barely able to lift him out of the back seat and carry him into the examination room. I set him down on the floor on his feet, hoping he might stay upright. And he did remain standing for a few seconds, looking at me for approval. But then he rocked back and forth, crumpled to the floor, and lay panting on his side.

When Dr. Elliott walked into the examination room a few moments later, I tried to explain what was going on. And, damn it, it happened again. I choked up, my eyes began to tear, and I couldn't speak. This was getting ridiculous. The nurse found my little display of emotion quite touching, which of course only made things worse. But all I could do was sit on the floor and hug Simba's giant head.

After that very awkward display, I was left with the inescapable conclusion that I loved this dog deeply. And not like any other pet I ever had. In my late thirties and early forties, I had a pair of Labradors, Fred and Ginger, who lived a reasonably long life and eventually passed away. And I shed a few tears in their memory. But with Simba, my fear for his life was far more visceral, like something you might feel for a close friend or even a child. Apparently, after spending nearly a decade together, all day, every day, Simba and I were bound together. And sitting on the floor in the vet's office crying, I was afraid that this bond might be broken.

With the help of powerful antibiotics and high-calorie dog food, Simba gradually recuperated from his still unidentified snout infection. And over the course of the next two or three months, he regained most of the weight he lost during his illness. But after any serious ailment, very old dogs, like very old people, seldom regain the same level of well-being they enjoyed before their health crisis occurred. And when the next illness strikes, which it inevitably does, they usually rebound to a lower plateau. This pattern repeats itself until the old person or the old dog in question is struck by an infirmity—maybe a broken hip or some sort of sepsis—from which he or she can no longer recover. And at that point, it's game over.

So three weeks after Simba collapsed in the driveway, he began eating his regular food again. But sometimes he left half of it in the bowl. And when Laureen got home from work, he no longer ran to the top of the steps to greet her. He just lay on the family room rug, smiling and thumping his tail on the floor until she came to see him. And once or twice a week, as he arthritically shuffled around the house, he would stumble and slump to the floor. Then he would look terribly sad and embarrassed as he struggled to pull himself up. And he would glance over at me to make sure I still loved him and still wanted him to be part of my pack.

Whenever that happened, I would rub his neck and reassure him as best I could. But Laureen and I both knew that his pattern of decline was now in place. And we girded ourselves for the day, perhaps not that far off, when we would once again drive thirteen-year-old Simba to Tamalpais Pet Hospital, and he would not return.

Laureen also had a pattern, but hers was an upward spiral. She would start a new job—like general counsel of McKesson—and in the early stages of that job, she would live in a constant state of low-grade fear convinced that somehow she'd fail. Harnessing that fear, she would work like a maniac—up to fourteen hours a day, seven days a week—mastering the task at hand. For the next year or two, she would learn the basics, then the subtleties, of her new position. She would become a superstar for five or six years. And finally, near the end of the cycle, beset by creeping boredom, she would scan the horizon for higher mountains to climb.

But seven years into her stint at McKesson, Laureen no longer had to search for higher mountains because the mountains were searching for her. Head lawyers of very large publicly traded companies possess a rare skill set, and there's no substitute for their experience. At any given moment, more than a hundred different individuals, corporations, and government agencies are either suing or threatening to sue the McKesson Corporation, with wildly different prospects of success. The first time the Justice Department slams your company with an $800 million demand or a plaintiff's law firm files a $15 billion bet-the-company class action suit, it's understandably alarming. The third or fourth time it happens, you kind of know what to do. So once you land your first general counsel job at a Fortune 50 company—and if you manage to survive four or five years, which many GC's don't—you tend to get a lot of job offers.

That was certainly true of Laureen. Every three months or so, a corporate recruiter fronting a gigantic corporation with a household name would discreetly contact her and invite her to switch teams. Laureen had genuine affection for her colleagues, and seven years into the job, she remained grateful to the CEO who had plucked her from mid-level obscurity. She also had faith in her company's future. McKesson was a tightly run ship with a gifted skipper. And like most health-care companies, it profited mightily from the twin tailwinds of Obamacare and an aging population. McKesson's surging stock price meant that Laureen's compensation now exceeded her dreams. So even though she was always flattered by the attention and occasionally pictured herself as head lawyer of a more widely known corporation, she would always mull the prospect over for a few weeks and decide to stay put.

But then one day, Laureen took a call from a recruiter representing Manhattan-based American Express Corporation—a company she had always admired in a city where she had always wanted to live.

Actually, it was American Express's second shot at her. Six months earlier, Laureen had politely listened to their headhunter's pitch and briefly considered a more challenging, more prestigious position in the white-hot center of the business universe. But at the time, she was bogged down in a long, complex acquisition, and there was no way she could leave before the transaction was completed.

Laureen assumed that American Express would just jump to the next candidate—which is what usually happened in these cases—and she was occasionally wistful about the lost opportunity. But this time, a top American Express executive convinced his CEO that Laureen was the best person for the job and that they should take one more crack at her. So when the headhunter circled back, Laureen knew it was serious business. And for the first time since she joined McKesson back in 2000, she agreed to engage in a "hiring process."

Needless to say, this turn of events threw our nicely settled household into turmoil. After seven wonderful years in Tiburon, we had finally gotten everything just the way we wanted it—or at least that's how it felt. Only that month, we had finally finished landscaping our Tiburon house. And up at Sea Ranch, we had recently converted our garage into a bunkroom so there would be plenty of room for our theoretical grandchildren.

And of course there was much more than real estate to consider. Over the last twenty-five years, I had developed a wonderful circle of friends in San Francisco and Marin County. We had watched each other's children grow up, graduate from high school then college, and in a few cases, start families of their own. We celebrated holidays and marked the milestones of our lives together. A quarter century of shared history isn't something you just walk away from. And it seemed highly unlikely that I would be able to develop a similar circle of friends in Manhattan—not at my age.

And it wasn't just me. Angela was in her sophomore year at a high school that was a remarkably good fit for her—an institution that nourished her intellectual curiosity, rewarded her diligence, and was full of other proto-intellectual nerds just like her. Hell, we even had season tickets for the San Francisco Giants who had won two of the last four World Series. So the idea of trading our well-settled lives in comfy casual Marin for an amorphous set of scary unknowns in dirty, noisy, dog-eat-dog Manhattan was disconcerting, to say the least.

Even Laureen was conflicted. Deep in her bones, she wanted to climb the higher mountain and finish her career at a globally known company. But she also felt deeply guilty about the disruption her fierce ambition might wreak on the rest of the family. So she decided the only way she could proceed in good conscience was to make her case to the family and take a vote.

Well, it wasn't precisely a vote. As you might expect from a big city lawyer, the referendum was more complex. Since Angela, Grace, and I would actually have to pull up stakes and move to Manhattan, Laureen granted us full veto power. Ostensibly, if any one of us objected to the move, then the whole deal was off. Kara, Will, and Lucas didn't really live with us anymore, and they wouldn't have to relocate. So they were cast in more of an advisory capacity. They could offer their opinions, but they couldn't block the move on their own. As a seasoned trial lawyer who went a career 40–0 in the courtroom, Laureen was probably pretty confident that she would prevail. But her offer to stay put if she didn't seemed substantially sincere.

Laureen approached me first, but I was a pushover. I had made my decision seven years earlier when Laureen ditched her own well-settled life in Atlanta to marry me. I gave her an IOU then. And I felt, if not thrilled, then at least obliged, to redeem it now. Laureen worked incredibly hard. And the rest of us benefitted from that. So if this was something she had to do, then I would support her.

"I want you to be honest with me," Laureen said one evening after dinner. "If I go ahead and take the job and we move to New York, are you honestly going to be okay with it?"

"Well, you know how much I love San Francisco and all my friends here," I replied. "So of course, I'd rather stay."

Laureen's face dropped a bit.

"And I'm not particularly ambitious—at least not the way you are. I was reasonably well-known in my field and set up financially by the time I was thirty-two, so I've had a lot of time to figure out that more money and more prestige don't make you any happier—not at a core level. But that being said, I've always been adventurous. And moving to Manhattan seems like an adventure I can still handle. So, like I told you seven years ago, if this is something you really want to do, then I'm right behind you."

Of course, from that point on, I had to listen to Laureen describe the move as "an adventure" every single time we discussed it. But, hey, once a trial lawyer, always a trial lawyer.

Twenty-six-year-old Kara also backed the move from the start. After graduating from Berkeley with a very impressive if not particularly marketable philosophy degree, she had signed up for some sort of advertising graduate school that I didn't know existed until I was asked to pay for it. Then she landed a job as a so-called "creative" at a hip Manhattan advertising boutique. Kara loved New York, her job, and family life in general, so the prospect of her clan, or at least the greater part of it, joining her in the Big Apple truly delighted her.

"Bring it on," she said.

Will and Lucas didn't seem particularly concerned about the whole fandango one way or the other. Will had graduated with a combination engineering and business degree from Cal Poly and worked in the data security practice of a huge San Francisco business consultancy. Data security was a red-hot space. So as usual, Will had landed in the right place at the right time. He did seek our assurance that we wouldn't offload his bachelor pad up in Sea Ranch. But once that critical issue was put to bed, he gave us his blessing.

Easygoing Lucas was savoring his college years in sunny beachside Santa Barbara and interning at a local tech startup. Lucas had always been a glass-half-full kind of kid. So we weren't particularly surprised when he said that he would be just as happy spending his school vacations in New York as San Francisco.

Grace, of course, had a lot more skin in the game. At fourteen, she was in her final year at a K–8 girls' school in San Francisco. Her classmates were about to scatter off to a dozen different high schools and boarding schools anyway. So for her, the timing was perfect. Plus Grace had always been a big-city girl at heart. She loved visiting New York with her mom. And once a year, she sampled the city's top gourmet fare with her biological father, Guenter the Chef (now rebranded "Günter"), who had moved to Manhattan with his third wife and late-in-life baby a few years earlier. So theoretically at least, Grace would get to see more of him. Grace easily adapted to new situations and was ambitious like her mother. So the prospect of a life lived on a larger stage appealed to her.

And then there was feisty, headstrong Angela.

So to be clear, Angela absolutely, positively did not want to move—uh-uh, no way, not going to happen. Angela is as deeply rooted as they come. And from birth, she has regarded any major change as anathema, particularly if it is imposed upon her from above. She is also a genuine introvert—in some ways still the little kid who trembled at the thought of attending a birthday party. So the idea of starting all over again at a brand new high school in a brand new city as a complete stranger—in the eleventh grade, no less—authentically horrified her. And to be fair, she had a point. But just as Laureen didn't want to be perceived as the hyper-ambitious mother who callously yanked her introverted child out of a high school she truly loved, Angela didn't want to be seen as the ungrateful daughter who stood petulantly between her mother and the job that would crown her career.

So Angela hatched a scheme. First she calculated that this time would be no different from the last several times her mother had contemplated a new job. Sure Laureen would be excited by the shiny new prospect. And sure she would discuss it in animated tones for weeks. But Angela figured that her mother would eventually decide to stay put—just as she always had. So when Laureen asked for her blessing, Angela disingenuously signed off on a plan that in her considered opinion had almost no chance of materializing. That way she would look like a team player but could still stay in Marin. From a sixteen-year-old's point of view, it must have seemed foolproof. But in reality, Angela underestimated just how badly her mother wanted this particular job. And when she failed to exercise her veto, the move to New York became a *fait accompli*.

But it took Angela a very long time to recognize that fact. Every evening when we sat around the dinner table discussing the move, Angela would say dismissively, "We're not really moving, so why are we even talking about this?"

And when we all flew to New York to look at schools, Angela very confidently told me, "Believe me, David. This is *not* going to happen."

And when we cruised around Manhattan looking for an apartment, Angela hung back at the hotel doing her homework because, and again I quote, "We're not really moving, so why should I waste my time?"

But then, after several months of clandestine meetings, Laureen gave her notice at McKesson and formally accepted the position at American Express. Then she packed her outsized wardrobe, bid the family a fond farewell, and boarded a plane for New York. At that point, Angela finally got the picture. And, believe me, she was not happy. Angela was angry at the situation in general and at herself in particular for not putting the kibosh on this whole crazy business back when she had the chance. And although she occasionally made a half-hearted attempt to appear slightly less than miserable in front of her mother, she was clearly terrified by the prospect.

The only way I could talk her off the metaphorical ledge was by making her a promise I hoped I would never have to keep. Namely, that if she sucked it up and moved to New York with a half-decent attitude and a whole lot less complaining, then someday, maybe a year after Simba's eventual demise, we would buy her a pug—a ludicrous breed of tiny dog with which she had become inexplicably obsessed. And by obsessed, I mean she would literally run down the street yelling, "A pug! A pug!" every time she saw one.

"Would that do it?" I asked her one Sunday morning over bacon and eggs in a Sausalito coffee shop. "If we promise to buy you a pug after Simba dies, would that make the move to New York more palatable to you?"

Angela gave me one of her famously skeptical stink-eye looks, and asked, "Are you serious, David?"

"Dead serious," I replied. "Provided, of course, you keep your end of the deal."

A smile spread across Angela's face—one of the few I'd seen in recent months. She looked me straight in the eye, nodded her head and said, "Yep. That would do it."

So even though I didn't really need one, I now had yet another reason to hope that Simba would live on—at least for two more years when Angela would leave for college and she could get her own damn pug. In the meantime, I hoped the mere prospect of a pug puppy in the big city would help Angela make peace with her plight—and to a large extent, it did.

Of course, we didn't tell Simba about the pug. Nobody wants to contemplate his own demise, let alone his successor. Plus the idea of replacing a big strapping hound like Simba with a twenty-pound gargoyle that resembled a cross between a pot-bellied pig and a rhesus monkey seemed like nothing short of blasphemy.

Nor could we discuss with Simba his imminent relocation from our sunny wooded acre in Marin to a comparatively small apartment in the concrete heart of a cold, noisy city. All Simba knew was that Laureen left home after the long Fourth of July weekend and never returned. Then the girls took off a month later, and they didn't come back either.

Despite his conspicuous courage in nearly all other arenas, Simba had always suffered from separation anxiety. Fortunately it was seldom an issue. With seven family members, extended family, and the kids' friends running in and out of the house all day—not to mention the fact that I worked at home—Simba was almost never alone. And whenever he did find himself unattended for a few hours, he seemed to embrace the notion that occasionally it would be his duty to hang back and guard the fort.

Still, Simba became visibly upset every time he saw suitcases in the front hall, because he knew that meant one or more of his pack members would be leaving for a while. And once a year, when the whole family traveled to Tahoe, and we all went out to dinner, leaving him alone in a strange rental property, Simba would sometimes brood for a while and then vomit on the rug. One of the few insoluable glitches in the glorious human-canine relationship is that there's simply no way to tell a dog how long you'll be gone or to reassure him that you will eventually return. So when you walk out the door with a suitcase in your hand, dogs tend to worry.

Simba didn't throw up when Laureen and the girls left for New York. But he did seem a bit depressed that his pack had dwindled down to just the two of us. Laureen and I had decided to keep our home in Tiburon for a while—just in case things didn't work out as well as expected. So when Laureen and the girls took off, Simba and I stayed back to close up the house and clean out all the closets, cupboards, and drawers. I also had to deal with several sets of movers who came by to pick up all of our clothes, ten cases of California wine, and three or four paintings we wanted to hang in our big city apartment. All of that involved moving dozens of suitcases, boxes, and crates out of the house, which was exactly the sort of commotion that upset Simba. That mental stress, combined with a sleepover at the vet's when I went out of town for four days, likely caused Simba to contract an ailment called kennel cough.

Simba had been inoculated against kennel cough, which is essentially the canine version of bronchitis. But he got it anyway. And that was worrisome for two reasons. First, Simba's advanced age and recent snout infection made what is usually a manageable illness significantly more dangerous. And second, Simba might not be healthy enough to fly to New York in two weeks when we were scheduled to join Laureen and the girls.

Simba's longtime vet, Penny Elliott, had recently retired from Tamalpais Pet Hospital. So when I brought him in for his appointment, we met her replacement, a slim middle-aged Australian woman named Shay Redfield. That particular afternoon, every canine examination room was occupied, so Simba and I conferred with Dr. Redfield in a small cinderblock cubicle on the feline side of the practice. I'm acutely allergic to cats—nine on a scale of ten, one allergist told me—so to avoid the onset of asthma, I wore a blue surgical mask during the entire course of the consultation. That made the conversation we were about to have even more difficult.

"So how's he doing," I asked Dr. Redfield after she examined Simba with a stethoscope, peered down his throat, and drew some blood.

"Well, he does have bordetella," she replied, using kennel cough's official name, "But there's another more serious problem. Have you noticed any labored breathing?"

"Definitely." I replied, "Not all the time, but sometimes when he's just lying on the family-room rug he starts panting like this." I imitated a dog panting hard through the surgical mask. "I kind of wondered what that was. I thought maybe he was just excited about something."

"No. That's laryngeal paralysis," Dr. Redfield replied. "It's fairly common in old Labradors and other large-breed dogs. Basically, the larynx constricts and becomes inelastic, and that makes it difficult for the dog to breathe—more so with the bordetella."

"Is there anything you can do for him?" I asked.

"For the bordetella, yes. We can give him a course of antibiotics that should clear it up in three or four weeks. And there is a surgical procedure that can permanently open up the larynx. But at Simba's age, it doesn't make sense. Just putting him under would be dangerous."

So apparently this was like Simba's lumps. There was a simple fix, but he was too old to benefit from it.

"There's another wrinkle," I said. "Simba and I are moving to New York soon. My wife recently took a new job there, and she's already in Manhattan with the girls. Simba and I are supposed to join them in two weeks. Will it still be okay to put Simba in his crate and fly him to New York?"

"I wouldn't," Dr. Redfield replied. "That's a stressful situation for any dog, let alone a dog as old as Simba. And if you factor in the paralyzed larynx and the bordetella, it's doubtful he would survive the trip. In fact, you should probably get used to the idea that Simba won't be around very much longer." She glanced at his chart and added, "He's nearly fourteen. That's pretty ancient for such a big dog."

"So how much time does he have?" I asked, not really wanting to know the answer.

I expected her to say something vague like, "Well, there's no way to know for sure," or "It depends upon various factors," like doctors usually do. But I guess veterinarians are more straightforward than the doctors who treat humans because Dr. Redfield replied very plainly—though not unkindly—saying, "Honestly, it could happen any day now."

I lowered the surgical mask and thanked her.

"Alright," I said, "I understand. I need to talk to my wife. I'm sure we'll figure something out."

That evening I called Laureen, who was staying with Angela and Grace at a midtown hotel while our new apartment was being repainted.

"Bad news," I began.

"What is it?" asked Laureen, unflappable as usual, because in her line of work she gets at least some bad news every day.

"So, as you know," I continued, "Simba has been under the weather again. There's a new vet at the pet hospital. And she says Simba has kennel cough—which is already a problem. But there's another more serious issue. Apparently, he also has a paralyzed larynx, which I guess is fairly common in old Labs."

"What does that mean exactly?" asked Laureen.

I recounted what Dr. Redfield told me as faithfully as possible and then added, "The bottom line is that we can't put Simba in a crate and fly him to New York. The vet says it would kill him."

Laureen sighed. Yet another reason to feel guilty about the move.

"So I've been looking into alternatives," I continued. "And realistically, there are two. We can hire a commercial pet transportation service that will drive Simba from San Francisco to New York in three days. It costs around $3,000. But I checked with your new employers, and apparently they will reimburse you for that. The downside, of course, is that Simba would have to ride all the way across America in the back of a van with someone he's never met and who probably won't take care of him the same way we would."

Laureen paused for a moment and said, "That doesn't feel right to me. Separating Simba from everyone in his family right now is probably the worst thing we could do. If he's as sick as you say he is, he'll need a lot of attention, which he probably won't get from the driver."

"I agree. So here's the other alternative. You told me that you wanted to bring your station wagon to New York. So instead of shipping it across the country on a truck or a train, or whatever it is they do, why don't I just drive it to New York? And Simba can lie on his bed in the back with his food and water and all of his stuff. And I could pull over whenever he gets nauseous or looks like he needs a break. Basically, I would be with him 24/7, and we'd get to New York in a week or so."

Then I had to deliver the really bad news. "But here's the thing, Laureen. The vet said pretty clearly that Simba could die any time now. So if I do drive him to New York, he might make it, and he might not. So you have to prepare yourself for that."

In Laureen's mind, neither option was great. She obviously didn't want Simba to die all alone in the back of a van driven by a stranger. But she also didn't love the idea of me cruising across America with only Simba for company.

In my early forties—about a decade after I sold my little publishing company—I took my first wife and three young children—nine, eight, and three at the time—on a yearlong trip around the world.[2] During the course of that journey, I drove my family across several fairly large countries including France, Greece, Italy, and Australia. We also drove across India, but that actually did scare the crap out of me, so I hired a local driver. But the point is, Laureen didn't know me back then. So she didn't really see me as the entirely competent long-distance driver I was. She saw me more as the absent-minded suburban motorist who occasionally got into a close scrape in the Whole Foods parking lot and was once responsible for a rather expensive fender bender on Tiburon Boulevard.

So if Simba and I did drive across America, Laureen would likely worry the entire time. And since she was already worried about whether she would succeed in her new job, whether our apartment would be ready before school started, whether the girls were adjusting to their new life in Manhattan, and now thanks to me, whether Simba was going to live or die, pretty much the last thing she needed was an additional source of anxiety. It might just push her past her breaking point, which is exceedingly high but certainly not infinite.

"Let me think about it," said Laureen. "We still have two weeks before you leave. So we don't have to decide right now."

---

[2] The journey is recounted in my 1999 book, *One Year Off: Leaving It All Behind for a Round-the-World Journey with Our Children.*

The next morning, I drove ten miles north to the little nine-hole golf course where my old friend Erick Steinberg and I played every Sunday morning. One of the many wonderful things about the sublime game of golf is that you always have plenty of time between strokes to discuss whatever's on your mind. And in my case, there are always lots of strokes.

"You nearly packed?" Erick asked as we strolled down the seventh fairway.

"Yeah, pretty much," I replied, "and I'll tell you, Erick, I'm really going to miss our Sunday morning golf games. I have no idea how I'm going to play golf when we live in Manhattan."

"I'll miss it, too," said Erick. "But whenever you come back, we can always shoot a few rounds."

"I have run into one major problem," I replied. Then I explained the whole Simba dilemma, including the fact that Laureen didn't really trust me to drive across America by myself. Erick expressed sympathy for Simba. Then he paused for a beat and a big grin spread across his face.

"What are you smiling about?" I asked.

"Road trip," he replied.

"What do you mean?"

"Road trip!" he repeated more emphatically.

"Are you saying that you'd be willing to drive three thousand miles to New York with Simba and me?"

"Hell, yeah!" said Erick, "You and I have been talking about a boys' road trip for more than ten years. So why don't we just do it? And we'll get Simba to New York in the process."

"I guess we could head south and follow the old Route 66, which is essentially I-40 now."

"Exactly," said Erick.

We were on the same page.

"But you do realize, Erick, that Simba is on his last leg. The vet basically told me it was even money whether he'd make it to New York. And if he kicks the bucket out in Oklahoma or Kansas or somewhere, it won't be pretty."

"Then that will be our mission," Erick replied. "Come hell or high water, we will get Simba to Manhattan."

Erick was right. First Simba had to say goodbye to Will and Lucas in California. Then Erick and I had to get him to New York so he could see Laureen and the girls before he died. Simba had lived with Angela and Grace since he was an eight-week-old puppy and the girls were only two and four years old. Now Angela was a bright, articulate seventeen-year-old, and Grace, at fifteen, was an athletic, six-foot-tall beauty.

For as long as the girls could remember, Simba had been a source of immense joy and comfort to them. He enhanced their lives in countless ways. When they were sad, they hugged Simba. When they were happy, Simba jumped around with them. He was like a brother to them, only nicer. And if he died before they could say farewell, they would always regret it. And Simba wouldn't understand why his family wasn't there for him in his final moments.

And Laureen, raised on Catholic guilt, would of course blame herself for everything.

Plus, there was another more metaphysical consideration. At the end of the day, we all die, and there's nothing we can do about it. The vet already told me she couldn't help Simba anymore. And there was probably nothing I could do to forestall his death. But with Erick's help, I could at least reunite Simba with his family before he bid this world adieu. It would be an admittedly small victory in the face of a heart-rending loss. But if I succeeded, I could at least console myself with the thought that I did everything I could to give my old friend the best possible death. If the King of the Canines had to die—which he certainly did and probably soon—then he should at least do so in the loving arms of his family, not alone and terrified in the back of a dog-moving van. Making sure that happened was my sacred duty as his friend and companion. It was a simple matter of respect and, of course, love.

Erick not only framed the mission, he also made it possible. It was a well-established fact that Erick's wife, Lisa, would let him do pretty much anything he wanted provided he did it with me. And it was also true that Laureen cut me a lot more slack when I was with Erick. I haven't the slightest idea why Lisa would put so much confidence in me. It honestly seemed misplaced. But I do know why Laureen trusted Erick.

Erick is what you call a *mensch*, which in German just means "human being," but in Yiddish connotes a man of integrity, someone you can count on. The closest English equivalent is probably "stand-up guy." What's more, Erick is amazingly competent in the physical world. For most of his career, Erick designed, built, and maintained the sort of broadcast equipment used by commercial radio stations. And he loved everything about radio transmission, right down to the last kilowatt. In fact, one of his many nerdy hobbies was yakking on a state-of-the-art ham radio set with other ham radio nerds around the world. And for fun, he rebuilt old vacuum tube transmitters that he found online or at specialized flea markets.

But with the decline of commercial radio and the rise of all things digital, Erick was compelled to switch careers in his late fifties. And for the last several years, he had designed and engineered smart power grids for electric utilities around the world. That was impressive in its own right. But what it meant in terms of a road trip was that Erick could fix an engine or a flat tire or pretty much anything else that might conceivably break on a car. He could drive and navigate well, and I knew he was 100 percent dependable. I always called Erick "the world's most competent person." And although he's modest by nature, he never really objected to that characterization.

But even more essential on a three-thousand-mile road trip, Erick was pretty good company—this despite the fact that he didn't really talk that much—or maybe it was because of that. Either way, I knew that Erick wouldn't drive me crazy when we were stuck in a car together nine or ten hours a day for seven or eight days straight.

Now it was true that whenever you drove somewhere with Erick, he felt compelled for some reason to point out every single AM, FM, cellular, microwave, or any other type of cockamamie radio tower he happened to see along the way. And on a trip across America, that could mean hundreds, maybe even thousands, of such radio towers. But I figured that was a reasonable price to pay for Erick's companionship.

So with reliable, old, tried-and-true Erick onboard, Laureen was satisfied that I would have adequate adult supervision, and she approved the expedition. I gave Erick the good news. Then I spent the next several days tying up loose ends, buying provisions, and plotting our course.

Unlike the commercial dog van, we wouldn't sprint across America as quickly as possible. At first flush, a quick trip made sense. We were, after all, racing death. And if Erick and I just put the pedal to the metal and took turns at the wheel, we could probably make it to Manhattan in just over two days. But driving twenty-four hours a day—or even twelve hours a day—would likely take its toll on Simba and might hasten his demise. In my experience, Simba was good for three, maybe three-and-a-half hours at most in the back of a station wagon. After that, he needed a bathroom break and ten or fifteen minutes of just walking around in order to regain his equilibrium. Otherwise he would get carsick and make very disturbing gagging noises. And in his frail condition, I didn't want to push his limits.

And because we can't help but anthropomorphize our pets, I initially told myself that this journey would also be a wonderful opportunity for Simba to see America before he kicked the bucket. And oddly, whenever I mentioned that notion to family or friends, they would always say something encouraging like, "Yeah, Simba's going to love seeing all those amazing sights."

But if you actually think about it for more than a few seconds, you realize that dogs probably don't care very much about seeing America. To Simba, a roadside field in Tennessee or Kentucky—or Outer Mongolia for that matter—was probably pretty much the same as a roadside field in California. And I sincerely doubted that Simba—or any other dog for that matter—had a bucket list. But, hey, Labradors always like to sniff new smells and meet new people. So maybe Simba, who had always been gregarious and intrepid by nature, might enjoy spending his final days meeting the nice folks in Arizona or strolling through a cow pasture in Texas or pissing on a tree at Graceland.

In 1960, the celebrated American novelist John Steinbeck drove from Long Island to Salinas, California, and back in a camper truck with only his brown standard poodle, Charley, for company. Most of America's interstate highway system didn't exist in 1960. So Steinbeck drove, for the most part, along two-lane roads lined here and there with fruit and vegetable stands, antique shops, local bars and restaurants. In *Travels with Charley*, his popular memoir of the eleven-week journey, Steinbeck predicted that, "When we get these thruways across the country, as we will and must, it will be possible to drive from New York to California without seeing a single thing."

Needless to say, Steinbeck's prediction came true. And fifty years later, Erick and I could easily drive from San Francisco to New York without seeing very much at all—except, of course, hundreds of radio towers. But that seemed like a wasted opportunity. So as long as we were making the journey—and as long as we had to stop every three hours for Simba anyway—we might as well see some of what was out there. And if Simba lacked the capacity to appreciate our grand tour, he probably wouldn't mind it either.

Based on those considerations, the trip began to gel. Erick and I would loop across America's southern tier for seven or eight days depending how it went. We would overnight in Las Vegas, Nevada; Gallup, New Mexico; Amarillo, Texas; Little Rock, Arkansas; Nashville, Tennessee; and Pittsburgh, Pennsylvania, where, after a guilt-ridden six-month hiatus, I would finally visit my ailing parents. These cities were all between six and nine hours apart—so a decent day's drive, but not an endurance test and probably a comfortable pace for Simba.

Then on the last day of the journey—at least the way I imagined it—Erick, Simba, and I would bid Pittsburgh good-bye, ramble across Pennsylvania and New Jersey, triumphantly cruise into Manhattan, and pull up in front of our new apartment building on New York's Upper East Side. I would phone Laureen from the street. She and the girls would run out the front door of the building and joyously clasp Simba to their bosoms before he met his maker. And at that point, my duty to Simba would be fulfilled. According to this plan, we would leave San Francisco on Sunday, August 17th, and if all went well, we would cross the finish line on Saturday, the 23rd, or Sunday, the 24th.

Six days before our departure, I heard a helicopter hovering just above my house, then another helicopter, then a third, and a fourth.

I was used to seeing small planes flying low over our property. It's a scenic area, and private pilots like the view. But I couldn't remember seeing a helicopter up there before, let alone four helicopters at one time. I knew it couldn't be anything good—maybe a big brushfire up in San Rafael or a pileup on 101. I switched on the television, and the answer was on at least seven different channels. The iconic sixty-three-year-old comic actor Robin Williams, who lived just north of us, had passed away. The helicopters were news choppers taking live shots of his house, which now had several police cars parked outside.

Watching those initial news reports, I didn't know yet that Robin Williams had taken his own life or why. In retrospect, I guess it makes sense that so much high-voltage mania would have to be offset by some sort of compensating depression. Plus there were rumors circulating that he might have a degenerative brain disease. But even so, the fact that a human dynamo like Robin Williams could be switched off just like that, leaving only a black void in his wake, sharpened my current preoccupation with the fragility of life. I knew, of course, that Robin Williams and my old dog Simba had nothing in common except in my own mind. One just died. One would probably die sometime soon. But Robin Williams's sudden demise—so unexpected and so close to home—seemed to lend our journey a new urgency.

Our first day on the road would also be our longest. According to Google Maps, our Las Vegas hotel was 580 miles from my house in Tiburon. At an average speed of sixty-five miles per hour, that meant nine hours of driving. And of course we would have to stop every three hours for Simba. Lunch would probably take another hour. So bottom line, if Erick and I wanted to eat a decent dinner in Las Vegas that evening, which we certainly did, then we would have to hit the road by 7:00 a.m., 8:00 at the latest.

When the odious little alarm on my iPhone began chirping at five in the morning, I woke with a shudder and a nervous stomach. Despite the fact that I had traveled internationally for decades as part of my job, the simple act of locking up and leaving home has always flummoxed me. Maybe I have some sort of low-level OCD or something, but I always feel like I'm forgetting some crucial but unspecified detail. So I end up running around the house like a chicken with its head cut off double- and triple-checking thermostats, door locks, the alarm system, every window in the house, the stove, the toaster oven, the coffeemaker, and any other electrical appliance that could conceivably spark the calamitous house fire that always lurks in the back of my mind. Maybe it's because my boyhood home in Erie, Pennsylvania, actually did catch fire in the middle of the night—back when I was thirteen. And a dozen firemen tramped through the house and ripped out a wall with their axes before they got the blaze under control. I should probably talk to a shrink about that.

Anyway, this particular morning was much worse than usual, because in addition to the confounding mechanics of departure, I was disoriented by the notion that this time when I closed up the house and took off for New York, I had no concrete plans to return. Today it wasn't just a five-day business trip or a ten-day vacation. This time the locus of our family life would shift from one side of the continent to the other.

That realization sparked an unanticipated wave of nostalgia. And I started thinking about the fact that our blended family had celebrated eight Thanksgiving dinners in this house, eight Christmas mornings, eight New Year's Eves and fifty-six birthdays—sixty-four if you counted Simba. I started thinking about the big fights we had here and how we made up. How we celebrated good report cards, college acceptances, and middle school sports victories. How we cried when someone was mean to us at school or work. Or when a boyfriend or girlfriend fell out of love with us.

I remembered the stormy night when the thirty-foot plum tree in the backyard toppled over and we had to hoist it back up with a winch; the time the garage flooded and we had to rip up the concrete floor; and of course the time the drapery hangers pierced the fire sprinkler line in the dining room with an electric drill (and a torrent of pressurized water shot across the room and splashed off the opposite wall until Angela climbed a ladder and stuck her finger in the hole like the little Dutch boy.) In fact I remembered all manner of minor calamity that bedeviled this house over the last eight years. And now that I was locking up for good, I found myself weaving all of those wretched little mishaps—irritating, maddening, even frightening when they occurred—into a warm and wistful tapestry.

But most of all, I remembered a brief shining chapter in our lives when five beautiful children and their faithful hound, Simba, filled every room in this house with laughter, shouting, barking, blaring music, and slamming doors. A time when there was always someone at home so we never locked our doors. A time when no one ever returned to an empty house. A time that overflowed with the fullness of life. And I mourned the passing of that luminous episode.

Kara had been gone for six years now—first across the bay in Berkeley, now across the country in Brooklyn. Maybe we'd see more of her in New York—maybe not. Every two weeks or so, Will used to drive across the Golden Gate Bridge from San Francisco to have dinner with us. But now we might go months without seeing him. And this year for the first time, Lucas stayed down in Santa Barbara for the summer instead of coming home because now he had a year-round internship. A fuzzy image of Lucas as a cherubic, curly-haired, slightly cross-eyed two-year-old popped into my mind. Then with a burn in my gut, I felt him drifting away.

Nearly every person who has ever met my mother has used the same phrase to describe her—"a force of nature." But now that force had waned. My mother—still brilliant and articulate on the days when her brain got enough oxygen—was, for the most part, a feeble invalid, bedridden twenty-two hours a day with an oxygen tube stuck up her nose because her heart was slowly dying.

When my mother was first confined to her bed—after several bad falls and a mitral valve replacement that didn't really work because she refused to do the rehab—she asked me to call her every day. And I did that religiously. And nearly every day she would tell me in her raspy, gasping voice that as soon as she felt better she was going to hop on a plane and fly to San Francisco so she could visit this wonderful house one more time. And every time she said that, I enthusiastically agreed that when that day finally came we would all have a magical time. But we both knew in our hearts, hers slowly failing, that she would never come here again. And closing up the house and stashing away the wheelchair she used when she was here only put a period on that sentence.

Simba and I, both a little stiff so early in the morning, tottered down the bluestone steps to the driveway. Simba sat patiently on the concrete pavers while I backed Laureen's mom car, a gray Mercedes station wagon, out of the garage. I wore my khaki-green Elm Forks Shooting Sports cap, which I bought at this crazy five-hundred-acre gun range outside Dallas a few years earlier. I figured the cap might offset some of the soccer mom vibes emanating from the station wagon. And in my rich fantasy world, the bad guys out there on the road who saw me as an easy mark because of the mom car would think twice when they saw my shooting-range cap. I knew, of course, that all of that was complete idiocy. But I wore the cap anyway.

Six months earlier, Simba could still jump up into the back of the station wagon under his own steam. But that time had also passed. And Simba knew the drill. I opened the tailgate. He stood still as I lifted his front paws up onto the deck. Then he held fast as I boosted his hindquarters and pushed him forward into the car. Simba circled his bed three times as dogs always do. Then he lay down with a long, low groan, reminding me how much he suffered from arthritis. When the pain subsided, he let out a big sigh and looked up at me with his big brown eyes.

"Don't worry, buddy," I said, "I'm taking you to see Laureen and the girls."

Simba smiled and panted, just delighted we were taking a ride together. His pure guileless joy instantly offset all the maudlin thoughts crowding my head, and I thought to myself, "Is it any wonder we love dogs?"

I buckled my seatbelt, put the station wagon into gear, and didn't look back.

When I first resolved to drive Simba across America, I failed to consider certain fundamental aspects of the journey. For example, pretty much everyone knows or would at least guess that only a small fraction of America's finer hotels and inns would be willing to board a very large dog for the evening. But somehow that thought never occurred to me—not, that is, until I tried to book our first night's accommodation in supposedly-anything-goes Las Vegas.

I began by calling the Bellagio Hotel since I had stayed there before. The conversation began amicably enough. I booked two rooms—one for me, one for Erick. I gave the reservationist—that's what they're called—my credit card information. And at the conclusion of the transaction, I casually mentioned that I would be sharing one of the rooms with my faithful hound and I presumed that wouldn't pose a problem. But it did pose a problem—not only at the Bellagio but also at every other Las Vegas hotel I called. It wasn't long before I began each such conversation not with, "Hello. Do you have two rooms available the evening of August 17th?" but rather with, "Hello. Do you take dogs?"

I did speak to a few nice folks who responded with a cheerful "Yes, sir, we do." But eventually they all got around to the same unexpected question: "How much does your dog weigh?"

Apparently, the bright line between acceptable and unacceptable canine guests is precisely fifty pounds, which seems entirely arbitrary to me. I mean why would a scrappy forty-five-pound pit bull or a yappy ten-pound shih tzu be okay, but an elderly eighty-five-pound gentleman like Simba wouldn't? It didn't make sense. It made even less sense that some of these places would accommodate not one, but two, dogs provided their combined weight didn't exceed the magical fifty-pound limit.

Instead of asking, "How much does your dog weigh?" shouldn't they be asking, "Does your dog bark for hours on end every time you leave the room?" or "Will your dog attack the cleaning staff? Or crap on the rug?"

Anyway, I spoke to at least five reservationists and three of their supervisors, and I politely asked each of them how they could presume to discriminate against a sweet old dog like Simba. And each time I argued my traveling companion's case with a heartfelt eloquence that failed to sway even one person's opinion.

But then, on a website called BringFido.com, I found The Vdara Hotel and Spa. (I mean, seriously, who names these places?) Located in the heart of Las Vegas's relatively new and entirely gargantuan CityCenter development, The Vdara is a cozy little inn with 1,495 guest rooms spread over fifty-seven floors and 1.6 million square feet. But for me, the hotel's fundamental allure was its comparatively liberal seventy-pound canine weight limit. And that, I figured, was close enough. I mean it's not as if they were going to pull out a scale and weigh Simba—or at least I hoped not.

"He might be a little over seventy pounds," I told the reservationist in an entirely unnecessary outburst of quasi-honesty. And when she didn't object, I moved on.

Needless to say, certain conditions applied. Simba and I would have to stay in one of the hotel's "Deluxe Vdog Suites," which didn't appear—at least on the website—to be precisely what you'd call a suite. And if you factored in the $50 "Dog Fee," and a separate $75 "Dog Cleaning Fee," it also wasn't precisely what you'd call cheap.

On the other hand, the Vdara did promise to welcome my big fat Lab with a generous array of canine amenities that included a handsome black acrylic dog blanket embroidered with the hotel's ridiculous name, a plush doggie bed, and a goodie bag packed with some pretty fancy-looking dog biscuits and a cutesy chew toy. They also had an optional dog crate that wouldn't come anywhere close to fitting Simba—although I wouldn't want to draw attention to that fact. And there was an "In-suite Dog Dining Menu," which, if you think about it, might confuse guests from certain Asian nations. But honestly, I was so relieved that Simba and I wouldn't have to sleep in the car that I fairly leapt at the opportunity to fork over whatever sum of money these good folks deemed appropriate.

Then there was another issue. During the course of the last quarter century, I have been fortunate enough to reside in a scenic locale blessed with a remarkably temperate climate. San Francisco's average daily high temperature is fifty-seven degrees in January and sixty-seven degrees in August. And where I live, in southern Marin, no one has air-conditioning because there's rarely any need for it. So even though I absolutely should have anticipated the dog in the hotel problem, I might be excused for overlooking another crucial question, namely: What do you do with your dog while you eat lunch at a restaurant during the torrid month of August when a parked car quickly becomes fatally hot?

I know your dog can't sit next to you at the table like they do in some Parisian restaurants—God, I love the French—and I've seen enough local news broadcasts to know that the correct answer is not "crack the window." But I'm embarrassed to tell you that this predicament only occurred to me—or to "the world's most competent person" for that matter—when Erick and I stopped to eat our very first meal of the journey in Bakersfield, California, a workaday city of 350,000 residents at the southern end of California's agrarian Central Valley.

Bakersfield, gateway to the Mojave Desert, was exactly halfway between Tiburon and Las Vegas—so a natural stopping point. And we knew there wouldn't be much in the way of amenities—or civilization really—once we drove into the desert. But the preeminent reason we decided to enjoy the first meal of our very long journey in Bakersfield was that Erick fondly remembered a dish he once ate there called Buck's Chicken-fried Steak. And you can only get Buck's Chicken-fried Steak at Buck Owens' Crystal Palace—an elaborate restaurant-cum-music hall on Buck Owens Boulevard in Bakersfield, California. Chicken-fried steak combines two things I really like—pounded beef and deep-fried breading—so when Erick suggested it as a lunch option, I pounced all over it.

Apparently Bakersfield once was—and probably still is—the home of "the Bakersfield Sound," a down-home genre of country music that arose in reaction to Nashville's increasingly slick orchestrations in the late 1950s. The idea was that even if Nashville decided to go all Percy Faith with its lush arrangements and syrupy strings, Bakersfield would stay true to its twangy Okie roots.

The Bakersfield Sound's foremost practitioners, Merle Haggard and Buck Owens, were country music superstars in the late fifties, sixties, and early seventies. Haggard was born in a repurposed boxcar in neighboring Oildale, California—a remarkably on-the-nose provenance for a self-described country outlaw. And Owens was reared on a Dustbowl dirt farm on the Texas-Oklahoma border. But they joined forces in Bakersfield. And they made beautiful music, both separately and together. They also married the same woman, Bonnie Campbell—at different times, of course. But since they lived in a relatively small city and had no fewer than nine wives between them, there was bound to be some overlap.

Anyway, when old Buck shuffled off to country-western heaven in 2006, he left behind the Crystal Palace as a physical manifestation of his musical legacy. It was a clean, happy, family-oriented venue where practitioners of the Bakersfield Sound and other similar-minded country acts could sing their hearts out on a state-of-the-art stage while their fans scarfed down Cryin' Time Onion Rings, Oklahoma Nachos, and, of course, the aforementioned Buck's Chicken-fried Steak.

Why it's called the Crystal Palace I have absolutely no idea, because there didn't seem to be any crystal in evidence. Nor did it in any way resemble its Victorian London namesake. It looked instead like a handsome nineteenth-century western village—or at least a pink and blue Disney version of that. And it was set beside a remarkably large parking lot that was practically empty—which didn't strike me as a very good sign.

That whole summer, Bakersfield—and pretty much all of California—had suffered record drought and scorching heat—a point driven home by the dust devils Erick and I saw spinning across the Central Valley's fallow fields and a massive brushfire we witnessed as we pulled into Bakersfield. So when we rolled to a stop in the Crystal Palace's huge empty parking lot and threw open the car doors, it of course felt like a blast furnace. And at that point it became instantly clear, even to a moron like me, that leaving Simba in the car would be a highly irresponsible decision.

"Hey Erick," I said as the lightbulb finally snapped on, "what are we going to do with Simba while we eat?"

"Now that's a good question," Erick replied. "Why don't we go inside and ask them what people usually do with their dogs?"

The answer to that question, I quickly found out from a pretty young hostess in a cowgirl dress, is that they leave their dogs at home.

"Just how badly do you want this chicken-fried steak?" I asked Erick.

Erick's mouth said, "Honestly, it's really not that important to me," but his eyes said, "I've been dreaming of Buck's scrumptious chicken-fried steak all week." So I determined to make this happen.

I strode back across the sweltering asphalt and retrieved Simba's big aluminum bowl from the back of the car. Then I popped inside, found the men's room and filled the bowl with cold water. I located a wooden bench set in a shady section of the front veranda. (It could only be called a veranda.) Then using the compass app on my iPhone, I calculated the likely arc of the sun over the course of the next hour—just to make sure that Simba would remain safely in the shade while we were inside. I lifted one leg of the wooden bench, put the loop of Simba's red leash around it, set it back down again, placed his water bowl next to him, and told him I'd check up on him every fifteen minutes—as if that meant anything to him. Then

I marched back inside and triumphantly informed the pretty young hostess in the cowgirl dress that I had expertly managed the whole dog situation and that we now required a table for two and, more to the point, two orders of Buck's Chicken-fried Steak. To which she sweetly replied, "Oh, I'm sorry. We stop serving brunch at one."

I pulled out my iPhone again. It was 1:10. This was information I could have used ten minutes earlier. So I asked the pretty young hostess very politely—honestly, I did—why she hadn't bothered to impart that information when first we met.

"Well, you can still go inside and look at the museum next to the restaurant," she replied as sweet as pie.

And you know what? That's exactly what we did. And to tell you the truth, there was a whole lot of very cool stuff in there, including a life-size bronze statue of Buck Owens, one of Buck's trademark red, white, and blue Mosrite guitars, and what had to be the world's largest collection of *Hee-Haw* memorabilia—since Buck famously co-hosted that country-western TV variety show for more than two decades. And this being Buck Owens' elaborate shrine to himself, there was also a colossal trophy case filled with every one of his music awards, which let me tell you, was a whole lot of music awards.

Perhaps most impressively, there was a Cadillac convertible ingeniously mounted to the wall above the music hall's long bar—its tires pressed to the wall and its open top facing the stage. The 1973 Grand Ville had apparently been pimped out by a once-renowned Ukrainian madman named Nudie Cohn (né Nuta Kotlyarenko.) A former shoeshine boy and professional boxer, Nudie found his true métier wildly overdecorating both Cadillacs and glittery "Nudie

Suits" worn by country music royalty and the occasional rock star back in the day. Remember the garish lit-up cowboy suit Robert Redford wore in *The Electric Horseman*? Well, that was a Nudie Suit, and not even his most flamboyant effort.

The wall-mounted Caddie featured a huge pair of chrome-tipped longhorns above the grill and door handles fashioned from real pearl-handled six-shooters. And the car's buckskin seats were embossed with nostalgic tableaux of Conestoga wagons traversing the Western prairie and caricatures of Indian chiefs in feathered headdresses. Legend has it—and the legend may well be apocryphal—that Buck Owens won this charming grotesquery from Elvis Presley in a poker game or possibly on a bet. Maybe the bet was about who had the classiest Cadillac.

At any rate, we were only inside Buck Owens's fantastical Crystal Palace for maybe twenty minutes, and even then, I popped out once to see how Simba was faring. But now it was one thirty. And according to the Yelp app on my iPhone, Bakersfield was not the Sunday brunch mecca one might expect. So that left fast food.

I watch a lot of television. There, I said it. And I won't try to justify my déclassé penchant by telling you that this is the "golden age of television" or that some of the best dramas are now written for the tube. Because, honestly, I also watched a lot of television back when it was mostly crap. More specifically, I've always loved sitcoms. It's probably because when I was a kid my mom and dad both worked at our family furniture store and didn't get home until six or seven each evening. So instead of sharing my day with them, I turned instead to my very amusing television friends—Gilligan and the Skipper, Major Nelson and Jeannie, and those zany POWs at Stalag 13. Anyway, as a result of this shameful addiction, I've been pummeled with literally thousands of commercials for a chain of fast food restaurants called Sonic Drive-Ins.

Despite the fact that there are more than 3,500 Sonic Drive-Ins nationwide, there are no Sonics Drive-Ins at all in either San Francisco or Marin County, California—just as there are no Walmarts or Dunkin' Donuts—at least not yet. Years ago, when my oldest daughter Kara was fourteen, we sent her off to French camp in Minnesota. (Don't ask.) And one fine day, she and her fellow campers dropped by the local Walmart to purchase some French camp provisions, whatever those might be. Kara casually mentioned that she'd never been to a Walmart before. And based on that offhand assertion, her fellow campers concluded that she must be vastly wealthy—which she certainly was not, although she did revel in the notoriety for a little while.

But my point here is that Sonics, Walmarts, Dunkin' Donuts, Dairy Queens, and the like can only be found in The Real America, which, as any Real American can tell you, specifically excludes the city of San Francisco and the adjacent county of Marin. And since, like the immortal Steinbeck, I wanted to see some of "The Real America" during the course of our cross-country journey, I asked Erick if he wouldn't mind dining at a Sonic Drive-In. And as always, Erick was amenable.

According to their round-the-clock fusillade of commercials, Sonic serves plump juicy hot dogs topped with a vast selection of condiments, some very oddly flavored milkshakes (Oreo cheesecake anyone?), and a nearly infinite variety of super-sugary soft drinks that include, for example, Green Apple Slush with Nerds-brand Candy. That's right. They spike their slushies with candy. Sonic obviously didn't serve Buck's Chicken-Fried Steak, so a modicum of disappointment was inherent in the venture. But with so many thousands of locations across America, I figured, how bad could it be?

Well, it is conceivable that Erick and I stumbled upon the worst Sonic Drive-In in the forty-four states where the chain operates. And if that's the case, I formally apologize to what must be tens of thousands of Sonic employees for drawing a universal conclusion from one bad experience. But it has always been my understanding that a bedrock principal of every fast food franchise is nationwide uniformity. And if that's the case, I will henceforth hurl caviar and foie gras at the screen every time I see a Sonic commercial. Because the grub at this place made the simple fare proffered at our local In-N-Out Burger seem like the pinnacle of haute cuisine.

Sonic's one saving grace was its shaded outdoor eating area. And that's precisely what we needed for Simba. So Erick and I jumped out of the car and found a dirty metal table that we tidied up with a handful of single-ply napkins. Then I plunked Simba down next to us without asking anyone's permission and tried to very quickly and discreetly pour a cup of dry dog food into his bowl from a twenty-pound bag before anyone could tell me to stop. In my haste, I missed the bowl entirely, and hundreds of little brown Science Diet Active Longevity Senior Dog Food nuggets rattled noisily across the patio, which, needless to say, attracted a good deal of unwanted attention from our fellow diners.

"Oh, shit!" I said to Erick. "Is anyone looking?"

Erick just shook his head and smiled because it was pretty obvious that everyone was looking.

"Can I help you with that?" Erick asked as I bent over and attempted to scrape up a zillion tiny nuggets with my hands.

"No. I think I can clean this up pretty quickly," I replied. "Why don't you run interference if the manager comes out."

"I can do that," said Erick, who fortunately finds it amusing when I do really stupid things.

After I recovered most of the kibble—amazingly, without being ejected from the premises—Erick and I shouted our orders into a crackly intercom that apparently had an ESL student at the other end. And eventually we received our "food." It's rare that Simba gets a better lunch than I do, but as I consumed something vaguely resembling a cheeseburger and onion rings, I regarded his kibble with envy.

"I'm sorry, Erick," I said. "Maybe I've been spoiled by a bunch of fancy-ass San Francisco eateries, but does this stuff taste like crap to you?"

"No, it's fine," said Erick, who probably didn't want me to feel bad about bringing him to Sonic in the first place. "I'm sure we'll do better in Vegas."

"That I promise you," I replied confidently. But then I realized that I hadn't made our dinner reservations yet, so I would have to do that as soon as we got back in the car.

Honestly, I'm normally a pretty confident guy. And before we embarked on this journey, I never doubted my ability to get Simba to New York in a safe, comfortable fashion—particularly with the world's most competent person by my side. But if our very first meal on the road—which really should have been a simple, straightforward affair—was any indication of how the rest of the journey might go, I knew I would have to up my game.

8. DOG STAR

Bakersfield, California
Still August 17, 2014
3,032 miles to go

After our regrettable lunch and a brief sweaty walkabout with Simba, Erick and I scrambled back into the air-conditioned station wagon, pulled onto CA-58, and headed east into the Mojave Desert. We were still four hours and 280 miles from Las Vegas, and Laureen's unspoken doubts about my basic fitness to manage this enterprise were slowly creeping into my head.

Shake it off, I told myself. Sure, we bungled our first meal on the road. We arrived at Buck Owens' Crystal Palace too late for brunch. Then I may have put Simba at risk by tying him to a bench in ninety-five-degree heat. I scattered dog food nuggets all over Sonic's outdoor patio. And I made Erick eat truly appalling fast food instead of the one meal he most looked forward to during the entire course of our journey. So all in all, not a great start.

But, hey, this was only the first half of our first day on the road. And we probably just hadn't hit our stride yet. Admittedly we didn't have a lunch plan that wouldn't require us to eat fast food in the car every day. And I still had no evidence whatsoever that any hotels beyond Las Vegas would admit Simba. But, hey, we could figure all that out as we went. And the important thing was that Simba was tolerating the drive remarkably well—maybe even enjoying it—and he didn't seem to be getting any sicker. So I just needed to clear my head. And, honestly, the Mojave Desert seemed like a great place to do that.

I've always loved deserts. Back when I was doing my *Day in the Life* books in different countries around the world—and later when I circled the globe for a year with my first wife and our three children—I made it a point to visit at least nine different deserts on four continents. Admittedly I only drove a car through most of those deserts or at most hiked around for a few hours. (I'm not really the hiking type.) But from that limited perspective, I've always found deserts to be serene, unsullied places with huge azure skies, rock formations that shift hues with the angle of the sun, and otherworldly flora you can't see anywhere else. Remember the epic 1962 David Lean film, *Lawrence of Arabia*? Well, at one point in the movie, a journalist asks Lawrence why he loves deserts. With a maniacal glint in his eye, he hisses, "It's clean."

And that's sort of how I feel.

At any rate, if you like deserts, you'll love the Mojave with its low-slung, pewter-gray mountain ranges, wide-open vistas, and thousands upon thousands of gnarly Joshua Trees. No wonder Jim Morrison and the rest of the Doors puttered out here in a VW microbus seeking enlightenment with a baggie full of peyote buttons. The desert gives you room to think. Or as the 1970s rock band America put it, in perhaps the most inelegant song lyrics ever penned, "In the desert, you can remember your name, 'cause there ain't no one for to give you no pain." And now that Erick and I were cruising across the Mojave, there weren't no one for to give us no pain either.

As we whisked eastward on CA-58, then northeast on I-15, it was comfortably cool inside the air-conditioned station wagon. But when I touched the passenger side window, it was nearly hot enough to burn your fingers. It was obviously sweltering outside, but we didn't know precisely how sweltering until we reached the aptly named hamlet of Baker, California (pop. 735).

The tallest structures in most communities usually offer clues to their defining characteristics or centers of power. Until the last century, the tallest structure in many European cities was the local Roman Catholic cathedral because the Holy See was much of Europe's dominant institution for centuries. In New York—a town more inclined to worship filthy lucre—the tallest buildings house mighty financial firms and, in recent years, the sprawling aeries of the rich and famous. But the tallest structure, by far, in tiny Baker, California, was a 134-foot-high thermometer erected in 1991 to celebrate the town's torrid climate, and more specifically, the world record 134-degree temperature recorded in nearby Death Valley just over a century ago. (Baker's own record high, notched in 2007, is a paltry 125.)

Apparently, what's billed as the "world's tallest thermometer," and very likely is, had been switched off for the past two years because the electricity needed to illuminate it had proven too costly. (If there was ever a case for solar conversion, this had to be it.)

But luckily for Erick and me, the widow and daughter of Willis Herron, the thermometer's visionary creator, had recently plunked down enough scratch to repaint the local landmark, replace its incandescent bulbs with cost-efficient LEDs, and switch this towering testament to torridity back on again. And that's how Erick and I knew that it was precisely 111 degrees Fahrenheit when we pulled into Baker to refill our tank and tend to Simba.

I thought it was hot in Bakersfield. But there's a palpable difference between 95 degrees and 111 degrees. In fact, it was so shockingly hot outside we weren't sure we should let Simba out of the air-conditioned car at all. After we topped off the gas tank, Erick and I bent over and felt the asphalt with our hands to determine whether it might burn Simba's pads. It clearly would. But one look into Simba's rheumy brown eyes told us that the dog had to go—and sooner rather than later. So we handled it like an Indy pit stop.

I drove the station wagon onto a patch of dusty ground adjacent to the gas station. Then we lifted Simba out of the car straight onto the dirt, which was hot, but not nearly as hot as the asphalt. At first Simba looked stunned. His eight years in Tiburon had been a balmy cavalcade of warm days and cool nights. So he had never felt anything like this, even during his sultry Georgia puppyhood. I was initially worried that the sudden surge of heat might overwhelm old Simba and cause him to faint. But after the initial shock subsided, he literally shook it off and promptly took care of business. Then Erick and I lifted him back into the car in the usual fashion. And the whole process took less than a minute. Simba still needed a proper walk, but that would have to wait until Las Vegas, which made me wonder how hot it might be there.

In addition to the "world tallest thermometer," there were two other notable points of interest on the road from Bakersfield to Las Vegas. The first was a standard green and white highway sign that marked the exit for the fabulously named Zzyzx Road (pronounced "Zy-ziks"). If taken, the road terminates in the tiny settlement of Zzyzx, California. You may be asking yourself now, as we did then, why any place on Earth would be named Zzyzx. And I now know the answer to that question.

It seems that back in 1944, an enterprising radio evangelist and itinerant Alabama con man named the Reverend Curtis Howe Springer filed a mining claim here with the Bureau of Land Management. And on the strength of that slender assertion, he took it upon himself to change the name of this former wagon stop from Camp Soda Springs to the much more memorable Zzyzx—his thinking being that Zzyzx would always be the last place name listed in any atlas ever published. Then Springer bused in a work crew of semireformed drunks and derelicts from a skid row mission he operated in Los Angeles. And they very quickly and altogether illegally erected the Zzyzx Mineral Springs and Health Resort—an institution that Springer touted as "The Last Word in Health." (Get it?)

Springer prospered in his remote desert outpost for three full decades, selling drinks to thirsty travelers, advertising a "natural hot springs" that was only hot because Springer heated it with a large hidden boiler and, most of all, by peddling Zzyzx-brand patent medicines that claimed to cure everything from baldness and hemorrhoids to various types of cancer. By the early 1970s, Zzyzx could boast a sixty-room motel, an airstrip (called the Zyport, of course), an AM radio station, and an evangelical church where Springer preached the gospel and, needless to say, solicited contributions from the faithful.

But then as con artists, even talented con artists like Springer, are wont to do, he took things one step too far, selling building plots around the health spa to some of his wealthier patrons. As you might imagine, selling government-owned land to well-heeled marks tends to attract the wrong sort of official attention—particularly when the marks in question tried to record their deeds at the local courthouse. And once the feds wised up to Springer's assorted scams, they seized his beloved Zzyzx and tossed Springer in the hoosegow on charges ranging from false claims and fraud to squatting on federal land.

Springer must have had a very good lawyer because in addition to the land seizure, he drew only a sixty-day jail term. And in the end he served only forty-nine of those days. Upon his release, Springer retired to Las Vegas—a town that has always appreciated a good con man. And until his death in 1985, he proudly maintained to all who would listen that he was and ever would be the rightful Lord of Zzyzx.

It's a good story. But I do realize that the Reverend Curtis Howe Springer bamboozled thousands of hardworking folks with his radio ministry, his fake hot springs, and, worst of all, with his worthless elixirs. But every swindle has a silver lining. And in this case, the payoff was three-fold. First, the compound that once housed Springer's "health resort" has now been put to much better use by the California State University's Desert Studies Center.[3]

More remarkably, a series of man-made ponds that Springer dug and stocked with fish for his guests' enjoyment turns out to be one of the last remaining habitats of the critically endangered Mohave tui chub—a species of small fish that would have vanished from the planet had it not been for Springer's elaborate three-decade scam. And of course, there's the marvelous green highway sign that still bears Springer's magnificent neologism—a sign that incites a smile from nearly everyone barreling along I-15, including Erick and me.

The other astonishing vision Erick and I witnessed on the road to Las Vegas was splayed out across five square miles of barren scrubland in a wide desert valley just west of the highway. The recently opened Ivanpah Solar Electric Generating System, a so-called thermal farm, consists of 350,000 mirrors—you heard me—each the size of a garage door. The mirrors are arrayed concentrically around three forty-five-story towers topped with black cube-shaped water tanks. Apparently, the mirrors reflect and concentrate the desert sun in order to boil water inside the tanks. And the steam they produce drives turbines that generate enough electricity to power 140,000

---

[3] In a truly stunning display of *chutzpah*, Springer showed up uninvited to the inaugural ceremony, spoke to reporters, and vaguely took credit for his "donation."

homes—which seems like an awful lot of homes to me, but apparently doesn't justify the $2.2 billion ponied up by investors like Google and the U.S. Department of Energy.

As Erick and I gazed down upon the sprawling thermal farm at five in the afternoon, it was still pretty bright in the Mojave Desert. But the fiery desert sun reflected in a third of a million mirrors created a luminous aura called a "solar flux" that was another order of magnitude brighter.

The atmosphere above the mirrors looked as if it might ignite at any moment. And that concept is not as far-fetched as you might think. Because only a few days later, as Erick and I drove through Oklahoma, we learned from an NPR report that the solar farm's employees had begun to notice a truly disagreeable phenomenon. Namely, that birds inadvertently flapping their way through the 900-degree solar flux were abruptly bursting into flame and plummeting to Earth trailing plumes of dark smoke. The employees had taken to calling these unfortunate creatures "streamers." And depending upon whom you believe—the plant's operators or incensed environmentalists—Ivanpah's solar flux will incinerate somewhere between 2,000 and 28,000 birds annually.

Every form of energy generation and extraction—even so-called green energy—comes with an ecological price tag attached. But rarely does the bill present itself so flamboyantly—actually I'd say biblically—as flaming birds raining down from the sky.

At any rate, from Ivanpah it was less than an hour's drive across the southern Nevada desert to Las Vegas. And it wasn't long before we spotted, off in the distance, Sin City's enormous hotel-casinos rising like phantasms from the desert. Our destination for the day was finally in sight. And after our ghastly lunch, Erick and I were more than ready for dinner.

Before we embarked on our cross-country mission, I assumed that Simba would enjoy, or at least abide, cruising down the highway all day in the back of a station wagon. And I knew he would relish the round-the-clock companionship implicit in such a journey. But as I mentioned earlier, I didn't think he would care much one way or the other about the various points of interest we might encounter along the way. And of all the points of interest that we might encounter during the course of our three-thousand-mile trek, the last place I thought Simba would enjoy was glitzy, libertine Las Vegas. As I quickly learned when I tried to book our first night's accommodations, the Las Vegas Strip isn't really set up for family pets.

But what I failed to consider is this: so few people actually bring their dogs to the Las Vegas Strip that the few intrepid mutts who do turn up tend to attract the sort of attention normally reserved for yetis and unicorns. Bringing Simba to Las Vegas was like bringing a baby to an old age home, or a Dallas Cowboys cheerleader to a mining camp. From the moment his paws hit the pavement—which was hot, but not Baker hot—Simba was the star of the show and King of the Strip. Dozens, nay scores, of people we met during our brief Vegas sojourn were pleased, nay, thrilled to make Simba's acquaintance. And in a setting otherwise rife with artifice and illusion, scruffy-faced young men with their shirttails hanging out, twenty-something women in platform shoes and spandex mini-dresses, and grizzled old duffers in sandals and baseball caps were all delighted to meet a big, tail-wagging reminder of the humdrum life they came here to escape.

And every one of these folks seemed to have a beloved pooch they left at home when they packed their roller bags and jetted off to Vegas. And within ten seconds of meeting Simba, they would all rummage through their purses or shimmy smart phones out of their jeans so they could show me photos of Jake the beagle or Fluffy the Maltese or Brutus the Great Dane who faithfully awaited their returns.

"Check this out," they would say. "This is *my* dog back in Cleveland (or Kansas City or Sacramento). He's a cockapoo (or a Labradoodle or a German shepherd). She's staying with my mother (or my sister or…)." Anyway, you get the idea.

It was a poignant and revelatory experience. And the upshot was this: if ever you doubt the vast and benevolent role dogs play in America's family life, just bring your pooch to Las Vegas, walk him down South Las Vegas Boulevard, and let the love flow. If you bring him, I promise they will come.

And Simba, who was an aristocrat by nature and extroverted even for a Labrador, basked in the warm glow of their adoration—sitting, smiling, and wagging his tail for all comers. For Simba, it must have been like when movie stars or politicians first become famous. And they can't quite believe that everyone they meet wants to shake their hand or take a selfie with them—or in Simba's case, scratch his neck and commend his rugged good looks. During those first ambrosial days of fame, before it all becomes tedious and creepy—which I imagine it does fairly quickly—it's probably gratifying to know that everyone loves and adores you and yearns to make a connection. And it's even more wonderful if you actually like that sort of thing, which Simba clearly did. And it's most wonderful of all if, again like Simba, you are old and infirm and your days are dwindling to a precious few and everyone still wants to lavish you with love and affection. In Las Vegas, Simba was a god.

In the preceding chapter of this small book, I penned a few harsh words about the Vdara Hotel and Spa. How they had a stupid name. How they were going to make Simba and me stay in an overpriced Vdog Suite. And how they were going to foist an array of tacky dog-related amenities on me—that sort of thing. I now wish to retract every last word. Because I don't care if management decides to rename this place the Shit-dara Hotel and Spa and charge me double what they did. Because in a town not always characterized by generosity of spirit, the staff of the Vdara could not have welcomed Simba more warmly had he been the queen of England's prize corgi.

I do realize that some of their gushy hospitality was probably attributable to the unicorn effect. But if it was, I don't care. Because from the moment we rolled our dusty, bug-bespattered station wagon up to the hotel's front entrance and released the hound, every parking attendant, doorman, and security guard greeted Simba with a big smile and heartfelt joy. And then, as we waited in line at the check-in desk, each passing bellman—and there were many employed by a hotel this size—paused long enough to babble some baby talk at Simba and rub his big furry head. The polite and amiable desk clerk graciously ignored the obvious—namely, that Simba clearly exceeded the hotel's officially stated canine weight limit. And cynical me, the Vdog Amenity Package that I previously ridiculed actually turned out to be a useful and thoughtfully assembled gift.

But perhaps best of all, the Vdara Hotel and Spa maintained a well-groomed dog park across from the front entrance—a lovely patch of well-worn grass where Simba could relieve himself day or night. I hadn't noticed this particular frill when I scanned the Vdara's website back in Tiburon. But I couldn't miss it when we actually arrived because no fewer than a dozen hotel employees upon spotting Simba cheerfully cried out, "Hey, you know we have our own dog park."

Since Simba had so recently watered the scorched earth of Baker, we didn't take advantage of this amenity until after we checked in. But after that and before we went up to our room I used my newly acquired plastic key card to gain entrance to a verdant postage-stamp-sized paradise ringed by fifty-story hotels. Simba was still a bit stiff from lying in the back of the station wagon all day. So he limped around on the grass for a while and sniffed here and there before he let loose. Once that was accomplished, I took him on his Las Vegas walk of fame. And then we headed up to our Vdog Suite on the thirty-third floor.

The Vdara Hotel was only four years old, so the accommodations were clean and modern and as warm and tasteful as a 1,500-room hotel can be. But more to the point, a comfortable dog bed was already in place. So I gave Simba one of his chewable arthritis pills and the antibiotic he was still taking for his kennel cough. Then I poured kibble into his bowl and watched carefully to make sure he ate it. After that I dressed up for my own much-anticipated dinner with Erick. I pulled down the shades, turned off the lights, and led Simba to his bed. I gently spread the black acrylic V-dog blanket over him. And finally, with the earnest hope that Simba wouldn't become lonely or anxious while I was gone, I lay down next to him and stroked his furry back until he began to snore—at which point I tiptoed out of the room and very quietly closed the door behind me.

I met Erick in the lobby, and we took a cab over to the Venetian Hotel where—after a brief phone consultation with Günter the Chef—I had booked a table for two at Daniel Boulud's DB Brasserie. In my mind, this would be the one evening during the entire journey when I would be able to treat Erick to a few tattered vestiges of the epic road trip he had once envisioned—before it turned into a mission of mercy. I knew I only had three or four hours before I had to get back to Simba. But during that interval, I hoped that Erick and I would be able to enjoy a proper dinner, polish off a decent bottle of Burgundy, hit the blackjack tables for as long as my customary hundred-dollar venture fund held out. And then who knows what might happen because, hey, it was Vegas, baby!

Anyway, that was the dream. But in reality, when we sat down at our little table in the DB Brasserie, I couldn't help but notice that, like several other Vegas outposts bearing the names of celebrated chefs, the sparsely patronized restaurant was excessively large and decidedly over-lit—more like a gourmet cafeteria. Chef Daniel's eponymous flagship restaurant on New York's Upper East Side serves up, by nearly everyone's estimation, one of the finest dining experiences on Earth. But the Vegas branch was more of a mass-market enterprise, which I should have anticipated but found disappointing nonetheless.

And to be fair, my perception of our very competently prepared meal conscientiously served in a clean, well-lighted place was likely colored by my slowly but inexorably mounting sense of abject guilt. As Erick and I engaged in a pleasant conversation about our various children and how they were doing in school or at work and whether or not they had boyfriends or girlfriends, etcetera, the monologue in my head was running something like this:

> *How could I have left Simba all alone in a strange hotel room our first night on the road?*
> *Does he feel abandoned up there on the thirty-third floor?*
> *I wonder if he threw up on the rug.*
> *What if he gets sick and dies while I'm sitting here blithely nibbling duck confit?*
> *What would I tell Laureen and the girls?*
> *How could I forgive myself?*
> *I need to get back to the room **right now**.*

This spiral of self-recrimination persisted through dinner and dessert. And when Erick and I finally plunked ourselves down at one of the Venetian's bottom-end ten-dollar blackjack tables, it was almost as if I were trying to blow my hundred-dollar grubstake as quickly as possible so I could return to Simba's side where I rightfully belonged.

Whether it was self-sabotage or my complete lack of gambling skills, I'll never know, but I successfully relinquished my whole wad in less than fifteen minutes. Then I turned to my traveling companion and said, "Erick, you know I wanted this to be a great boys' night out so I could thank you for helping me with this trip and all. But honestly, I feel like I should be back in the room with Simba. I'm sorry to be a spoilsport, but I think I gotta bail."

Erick, ever the gentleman, understood or at least said he did. So we abandoned our theoretically epic night in Las Vegas and grabbed a cab back to our hotel.

When we pulled up in front of the Vdara ten minutes later, I jumped out of the taxi and trotted across the lobby to the elevator leaving Erick in my dust. I pushed the call button repeatedly and then fumbled with the keycard outside my room. With each passing second, I became further convinced that Simba was either in distress or already dead.

When I finally pushed open the door to my room, I could see from the light in the corridor that Simba was right where I left him. Then I heard him snoring, and a wave of relief washed over me. A thorough search of the carpet on my hands and knees in the dark failed to turn up any anxiety-induced dog vomit. So apparently my entire guilty panic episode was completely unfounded and actually pretty ridiculous.

I woke Simba up with a gentle nudge just to let him know I was there. He gazed up at me with his big brown eyes and smiled lovingly before he drifted back to sleep. Apparently the long car ride from San Francisco and his Vegas walk of fame had exhausted the old dog. And he hadn't even noticed I was gone.

Simba shook himself awake, dog tags jingling, just before five the next morning. He roused me in the process, and my first thought was, "Thank goodness. He's still alive."

I gave Simba a big hug and told him what a good dog he was. Then I fed him breakfast and snapped the red leash onto his leather collar. We took the elevator down to the Vdara's colossal lobby. The doormen greeted us in their usual chummy fashion. Then we shuffled outside in the predawn gloaming for Simba's morning constitutional.

On the way back to the room, I popped into the lobby snack bar for a tall coffee and a breakfast sandwich. Needless to say, one of the counter guys working the dawn shift had two Labradors at home. And the moment he saw Simba, he fairly leapt out from behind the counter so he could share a few dozen cell-phone photos and some riveting tales of their shenanigans. (I know. I do it too.) Erick, Simba, and I were back in the car by eight, and Erick took the first shift driving east out of Las Vegas on U.S. 93.

Our ultimate destination that day was Gallup, New Mexico, 435 miles due east. At just over six hours, it would be one of our shortest one-day drives. And the larger, more cosmopolitan city of Albuquerque was only two hours further down the road. But I wanted to bunk in Gallup for two somewhat dubious reasons: first, I loved its evocative name; and second, a hot tip. Honestly, I didn't know the first thing about Gallup—and as it turned out, I should have taken the time to find out. But doesn't the name Gallup, New Mexico, fairly reek of historical romance—like Tombstone, Arizona, or Deadwood, South Dakota? And doesn't it seem as if it would be a classic Old West town with three or four swinging-door saloons, a limestone-clad bank with Ionic columns, and a rough-hewn wooden railroad depot, circa 1894?

I had no idea whether any of that was true. But I've always been a big believer in serendipity, particularly as it pertains to travel. And picking a place to visit solely on the basis of its name has worked out pretty well for me in the past. Elegant Spoleto, Italy, nestled in the Umbrian foothills; the colorful Mekong River town of Luang Prabang, Laos, and the South Pacific paradise of Bora Bora immediately come to mind—and all three were enchanting.

The second reason I wanted to lay my head down in Gallup that evening was somewhat more substantive. When I immodestly posted a Facebook item mentioning that Erick, Simba, and I would be more or less retracing the old Route 66—the fabled "Mother Road"—from Kingman, Arizona, to Oklahoma City, a Time-Life photojournalist I knew from back in the day posted an intriguing response. He said that whatever other kicks we got on Route 66, we should definitely spend a night at the historic El Rancho Hotel in Gallup, New Mexico.

Apparently, old-time icons of the silver screen such as John Wayne, Spencer Tracy, and Ronald Reagan once bunked at the El Rancho while filming classic Hollywood Westerns in the picturesque environs. And like Buck Owens' Crystal Palace, the El Rancho was supposed to be a living museum packed to the rafters with vintage Navajo rugs, ornate Victorian furniture, autographed publicity photos from the forties and fifties, and the sort of obscure memorabilia that's always been catnip to me.

Again, taking travel tips from globe-trotting photojournalists has always paid off in the past, landing me in any number of offbeat locales. The best, I think, was a lovely farmstead off South Africa's spectacular Garden Route between Port Elizabeth and Capetown. There the kids and I were met at the front door by the estate's grande dame, who was improbably attended by a baby baboon in disposable diapers… and the little fellow was casually sitting astride a remarkably patient Golden retriever! Now that's something you don't see every day. And the kids and I wouldn't have seen it at all if I hadn't been susceptible to random advice from my photojournalist friends. So if you put the two together—romantic moniker plus well-informed travel tip—then Gallup, New Mexico, seemed like a no-brainer—at least until we got there.

As the Las Vegas skyscrapers receded in the rearview mirror, I was pleased we had selected Sin City as our first overnight stop of the trip. Honestly, it was fifty miles out of the way. And if the truth be told, putting Vegas on the agenda had very little to do with

Simba or our core mission. It was just a selfish desire to have one great boys' night out before we resumed our dash across America. But thanks to my guilty panic episode, our boys' night out had been a total bust. But good old Simba had one of his best days ever soaking up the tourist love on the Las Vegas Strip. So score one for serendipity.

Twenty-six miles down the road—just over the Nevada–Arizona border at a speck on the map called Last Stop—Erick and I couldn't help but notice a long, low-slung compound painted fluorescent yellow and ringed by a dozen large, brightly colored signs. It was apparently a combination restaurant, gas station, ATV rental office, and gun range—but mostly a gun range. And the largest of its many flashy billboards read:

BULLETS & BURGERS
SHOOT A 50 CAL. MACHINE GUN

Apparently, Las Vegas tourists who want to add a dash of violence to their sex and gambling can cruise out into the desert aboard a lavishly illustrated Bullets & Burgers van and engage in four or five hours of exuberant gunplay.

And they don't play with just any guns. Bullets & Burgers stocks more than thirty varieties of high-caliber weapons including .44 Magnums (when a .357 just won't do), the globally popular AK-

47 assault rifle, a Browning .50 caliber machine gun on a tripod (which, judging from the sign, is the main attraction), and, I kid you not, a fully operational grenade launcher mounted to the business end of an M16. The Browning, by the way, can pierce lightly armored vehicles and blow low-flying aircraft out of the sky—so not what you'd call a sporting weapon.

Bullets & Burgers also boasts a large collection of submachine guns, including gangster-style Tommy guns with their distinctive round magazines, and compact Israeli Uzis, the most ubiquitous submachine gun in the world for more than two decades. And just in case you think this heavily-armed playground only attracts gun nuts and Second Amendment enthusiasts, you should know that in terms of popularity, Bullets & Burgers ranks number two—I'm tempted to say with a bullet—amongst all 199 Las Vegas-area "Fun & Games" activities listed on the popular TripAdvisor website. And it's apparently considered good, clean fun for the entire family, including children as young as eight.

Unfortunately, some children as young as eight can't be fully trusted with a submachine gun. And about a week after Erick and I blew past Bullets & Burgers—me still wearing my stupid Elm Forks Shooting Sports hat—I was chagrined to learn that a sweet nine-year-old girl in a pink shirt and ponytail had lost control of her Uzi and shot her instructor—a father of four—in the head at point-blank range.

Don't get me wrong. As my hat clearly indicates, I occasionally patronize gun ranges myself. And I grew up in a blue-collar western Pennsylvania town where the first day of deer season was a school holiday. I'll further admit that I've taken both Lucas and Grace to an indoor shooting range near our house in Marin County. But they were fourteen or fifteen at the time, not nine. And they took a half-hour lesson from a trained professional before they squeezed off their first round. But far more germane to this discussion, they fired a dinky .22 caliber revolver, which has almost no recoil, not a nine-millimeter automatic that, despite what you see on TV, generally requires two adult hands to control it.

When it comes to guns and the Second Amendment, I guess we all draw our own lines. But putting a powerful automatic weapon in the hands of a nine-year-old child seems to violate, if not the laws of Arizona, then certainly the dictates of common sense. When I first saw the story on television, and then all over the Internet, I initially thought, "Hey, I know that place." But then, of course, I felt deeply sorry for the instructor's wife and his four teenage children. But most of all I felt sorry for the nameless young girl in the pink shirt and ponytail who will probably spend the rest of her life reliving a horrific incident she couldn't prevent.

I'm pretty sure you're still reading this book to find out what happens to Simba, not to be subjected to a random tirade about gun control. But as a father of five who occasionally enjoys shooting pistols at paper targets and shotguns at clay pigeons, may I humbly suggest—I'm talking to you National Rifle Association—that keeping automatic weapons out of the hands of small children is not quite the same thing as depriving all red-blooded Americans of their God-given right to bear arms—in well-regulated militias or otherwise.

Hey, I realize that all governments, including our own—sometimes especially our own—overreach from time to time. But honestly, NRA, the slope isn't quite as slippery as you incessantly make it out to be. And, like it or not, common sense actually has a place in this discussion. So you can pry that little nugget of truth out of my cold dead hands.

Okay, now that I got that out of my system—and likely alienated half of my tiny population of readers—let's return to the story. Because a little past Bullets & Burgers, Erick, Simba, and I left the low desert behind and began our climb into the northern Arizona high country that eventually reaches an altitude of a mile and a half above sea level.

Our first day on the road, including the Mojave Desert run, had been about as hot as possible—always above ninety degrees and well into triple digits in the desert. And except for the Central Valley's patchwork of irrigated farm fields, the drought-parched western landscape had been a desiccated shade of brown all the way from San Francisco's East Bay to Las Vegas.

But now that we were gaining altitude, the temperature gradually cooled into the low seventies, and the scenery grew progressively greener. Eventually the highway ran through vast stands of ponderosa pine in the Tonto National Forest. And I could occasionally spot a few tiny lakes—or maybe they were just ponds—off the side of the highway. There was obviously a lot more annual rainfall up here than there was anywhere we'd been thus far. But I didn't expect to see it all at once.

When Erick and I stopped for gas in Kingman, Arizona, I took the wheel. So I was driving when the sky turned an ominous shade of gunmetal gray. Then, ten minutes later, the heavens let loose. Since there's little if any precipitation in San Francisco between May and October—even in non-drought years—Erick and I were initially delighted to see fat splashes of rain slapping the windshield and rinsing the Mojave dust off the hood of our car.

But then, minute by minute, mile after mile, the rain fell progressively harder. And it wasn't long before the windshield wipers, even at their highest setting, couldn't keep up with the downpour. I'd only seen this sheer volume of rain twice before—once in my early twenties when I was caught in a hurricane on the west coast of Africa; and again, two decades later, when I drove into Oklahoma City during a terrifying thunderstorm that featured thousands of lightening strikes and 110-mile-per-hour winds.

I tried slowing the car down from sixty-five to forty to see if that might improve the visibility. But even then it was like trying to see the highway ahead through a waterfall. Other vehicles on the road were just colorful blurs, and it sounded as if someone were playing a drum solo on the roof of the car. This, I concluded, was a dangerous situation. But being a guy and all, I didn't want Erick to think that I lacked either the proficiency or the intestinal fortitude to press forward—even in the face of this apocalyptically proportioned deluge.

But then, after ten or twelve more miles of squinting through the windshield and not being able to see very much at all, my bravado frayed. And I began hoping that Erick might say something to the effect of, "Hey, maybe we should pull over for a while." So that it would be him, not me, who was throwing in the towel.

But, alas, when I glanced over at my traveling companion, he seemed entirely at ease with the whole 'Noah and the Ark' situation. And I knew he would never capitulate. So in an act of cowardice, I glanced back over my shoulder at Simba to see whether he might be upset by the storm—you know, like dogs are supposed to be. Because if Simba were scared, that would be a perfectly valid excuse—I mean reason—to pull over and comfort the poor old hound until the tempest passed. (Sadly, this is how some men think.)

But, nope, brave old Simba was just as relaxed as Erick, casually sprawled across his bed and seemingly oblivious to our imminent demise. And when I briefly caught his eye, he just smiled at me and panted. And I knew that the panting was due to his paralyzed larynx rather than any sense of dread.

When that craven plan collapsed, I gripped the wheel even harder and stared straight into the monsoon. And as I did, I began to tell Erick a few poignant details of my epic Oklahoma thunderstorm adventure. How the fierce gale blew big green highway signs right over backward. How marble-size hailstones followed hard on the rain. And how I was eventually forced to seek refuge under a highway overpass in order to avoid certain death—you know, that sort of thing. I did that not only to establish my foul-weather credentials but also to let Erick know just how bad it might get out here if the storm persisted and we failed to respect its majesty. After I made my case, I turned to Erick and said as casually as possible, "You know, Erick, maybe we should pull over. I mean just until this lets up a bit."

And that, I figured, should do it.

Erick pondered my suggestion for a moment, peered up at the angry skies through the moon roof, contemplated the road ahead, and I suppose did a few calculations in his head. Then he replied, just as casually, "Nah, I think we should keep moving. The storm seems to be blowing from east to west. So if we maintain our speed, we'll probably come out the other side of it fairly quickly."

"How could you possibly know that?" I asked, trying not to sound exasperated.

"Well," Erick said. "Sometimes I study weather patterns to determine how radio towers will be affected by various atmospheric conditions."

Oh, no. Not the fucking radio towers again.

"And I'm pretty sure," Erick continued, "that we're not in any real danger here. It'll blow over soon."

Which forced me to say, "Well, better safe than sorry."

And before Erick could utter one more logical, science-based word, I jerked the car off the highway and onto the shoulder.

At first, I was relieved to see that we'd ended up right behind another vehicle—a big gray SUV presumably piloted by a similarly gutless, I mean sensible, motorist. Cowardice, after all, loves company. But then it struck me. I hadn't been able to see the gray SUV at all until I zoomed up right behind it at a fairly high rate of speed. And I could have easily crashed into it. So maybe it would have been safer to keep driving after all—like Erick said.

But now the deed was done. So I switched off the engine. And Erick, Simba, and I waited in near silence for the storm to pass, which I'm chagrined say, happened no more than ten minutes hence—exactly as Erick predicted.

So, basically, there had been no reason to push the panic button. And I realized that my reaction to the rainstorm along with my hasty flight from the Venetian Hotel Casino the previous evening made not one, but two, unnecessary panic attacks in the course of a single twenty-four hour period.

"Jesus, " I thought. "You really need to get ahold of yourself."

10. WONDER DOG

Erick being Erick, I guess I shouldn't have been surprised. But it seems that prior to our departure my traveling companion had compiled a list of fascinating roadside attractions that we could visit whenever time allowed and the spirit moved us. But rather than share this touristy lineup at the outset of the journey, as one might expect, Erick demonstrated a real showman's flair by revealing the prospective stops only as they came into range.

It took me a little while to figure out what Erick was up to. But once I did, I realized that his system perfectly suited our cross-country partnership. Since Erick was sole keeper of the Wonder List, I never knew what the next stop would be or when it might occur. And that appealed to my spontaneous nature. Erick, on the other hand, knew exactly what was coming and when. And that gratified his engineer's heart.

So every time Erick smiled his slightly crooked smile and got a particular twinkle in his eye, I knew that he was about to reveal his next all-American wonder. And each time, just before he did, I raised my hand like a kid in school and made the same tired joke, crying out, "I know! I know! It's the world's largest ball of twine!"

In point of fact, the world's largest ball of twine is in Branson, Missouri[4], a full 140 miles off our charted course. So we probably wouldn't go there, even to justify the joke. But on a road trip this long—on Route 66 no less—it did seem somehow imperative to visit as many of the world's largest doodads and gewgaws as possible.

And in that regard, we were more or less successful. Simba did, after all, take a piss in the shadow of the world's tallest thermometer. And at one point, in the tiny Texas panhandle town of Groom, we were privileged to witness what Erick claimed was "the largest cross in the Western Hemisphere." Although maybe that shouldn't count because, (a) by definition, the Western Hemisphere is only half the world, and (b) the claim itself is hotly contested by at least four other very tall Western Hemisphere crosses. One of these crosses, the 198-foot-tall "Cross at the Crossroads" in Effingham, Illinois, was built only seven years after our Groom, Texas, cross, apparently just to grab the title—which, by the way, doesn't strike me as particularly Christian.

But whatever the actual facts of the case are, I vote for Erick's giant Groom, Texas, cross because

    a.   to the best of my knowledge, none of those other giant crucifixes are ringed by life-size bronze figures depicting all

---

[4] To be as evenhanded as possible, I really should mention that while "the world's largest ball of twine" is in Branson, Missouri, "the world's heaviest ball of twine" is in Lake Nebagamon, Wisconsin, and the largest ball of sisal twine (as opposed to nylon twine) is in either Cawker City, Kansas, or Darwin, Minnesota, depending upon whom you believe.

fourteen Stations of the Cross (not to mention a full-size replica of Christ's empty tomb);

b. no other cross is anywhere near the "Leaning Water Tower of Groom," which is exactly what it sounds like, but which, for some reason, hasn't garnered the same global acclaim as its famous leaning cousin in Pisa; and

c. it's nowhere near as creepy as the 1,056 wooden crosses—grouped in Calvaryesque threes—that line the highways of West Virginia. (And by the way, I'd be just as creeped out if someone had erected a thousand crescent moons or a thousand six-pointed stars.)

Anyway, after the somewhat-less-than-apocalyptic Arizona cloudburst, I manfully admitted to Erick that maybe his foul-weather strategy might have been superior to my own. And I vowed that going forward I would not lightly dismiss any advice emanating from the world's most competent person.

I revved up the car, pulled back onto I-40, and within a matter of minutes, Erick gleefully revealed the first of his three wonders of the day. It was… drum roll, please… Meteor Crater, approximately fifty miles east in… okay, one more drum roll… the middle of freakin' nowhere.

The reason it's called just Meteor Crater, instead of Meteor Crater State Park or Meteor Crater National Monument or some other equally august appellation is that this particular natural wonder is privately owned and operated—by the Barringer family of Arizona.

So, how does one family end up owning a 500-foot-deep, nearly-mile-wide meteor crater? It's a great story, actually. And it all begins in 1906 with one Daniel Moreau Barringer, Jr., a Philadelphia lawyer and Princeton-trained mining engineer who had already made his fortune in Arizona silver. That year Barringer publicly challenged the generally accepted wisdom—championed by the preeminent geologist of the day, G. K. Gilbert—that the crater in question was the caldera of an ancient volcano. Barringer was convinced that only a very large meteor crashing into the earth at thousands of miles per hour could have made this particular hole in the ground. More specifically, he calculated that the meteorite in question would have a mass of ten million tons. And based on fragments littering the crater rim, that it would consist almost entirely of extraterrestrial iron with a little space nickel thrown in.

That, by the way, is enough iron to build more than a thousand Eiffel Towers. And once processed, it would yield the modern-day equivalent of $6 billion in profits. So the meteorite was well worth finding—particularly back in 1906 when it was apparently acceptable to dig up, melt down, and monetize a giant natural wonder from outer space. And since a ten-million-ton hunk of iron can't just disappear in a puff of smoke, Barringer figured it had to be down there somewhere—either deep beneath the crater floor or maybe a little off to one side if the meteor had struck at an angle.

So like the Reverend Curtis Howe Springer of Zzyzx, California, Daniel Moreau Barringer, Jr., filed a mining claim with the U.S. Bureau of Land Management. But unlike the grifting Reverend Springer, Barringer was already a wealthy man and the scion of a prominent North Carolina family—not to mention Teddy Roosevelt's hunting buddy. So he was able to procure what Springer never did: a "land patent" granting his newly incorporated Standard Iron Company full right and title to the entire mile-wide crater and a good deal of surrounding acreage. So with official federal paperwork in hand, but apparently without a simple magnetometer—which was certainly available at the time and would have told Barringer that there was no colossal mass of iron anywhere in the vicinity—he proceeded to spend the next twenty-three years digging for his six-billion dollar meteorite.

As it turned out, Barringer was right, but only partially so. What is now known as Barringer Crater was indeed formed by a giant meteor that collided with the earth approximately fifty thousand years ago. And just as Barringer predicted, the meteor was made almost entirely of iron. But, unfortunately, Barringer and his mathematically inclined colleague, Benjamin Chew Tilghman, overestimated the meteor's mass by a factor of thirty-three. Which meant that upon impact the meteor weighed a mere 300,000 tons, not 10 million tons as they had calculated. And the key phrase here is "upon impact." Because when the meteor slammed into the earth's surface at more than 25,000 miles per hour, it released 2-½ megatons of energy—roughly 125 times as much energy as the Nagasaki A-bomb—and the giant meteor pretty much vaporized, spreading a fine iron-nickel mist and the occasional chunk of iron across the high-desert floor.

So Barringer squandered more than two decades of his life, nearly his entire silver fortune, and virtually all of his investors' money rooting around for an enormous hunk of iron that was never there. Eventually—and some might say belatedly—Standard Iron's board of directors consulted one F. R. Moulton, a renowned University of Chicago astronomer. They asked Professor Moulton where their ten-million-ton meteorite might be. And at what must have been a very uncomfortable board meeting, Moulton explained the whole meteorite vaporization phenomenon. At which point, the directors pulled the proverbial plug. Daniel Barringer died shortly thereafter—a disillusioned man of substantially reduced means.

But as with Reverend Springer's beloved Zzyxz, Barringer's Folly had a silver lining (as opposed, I guess, to an iron lining). Daniel Moreau Barringer did not save an endangered species of fish like Reverend Springer, but he did significantly advance humankind's understanding of meteor impact sites. In fact Barringer was the first person to conclusively prove that meteor impact craters existed here on planet Earth. And he is still widely recognized for his contributions to the field. In 1970, NASA even named an impact crater after him—albeit on the dark side of the moon.

Furthermore, Barringer's heirs—and he sired no fewer than eight children—ended up owning a rather large swathe of remote Arizona scrubland that featured by nearly anyone's estimation a pretty spectacular hole in the ground. So with an eye toward posterity, they decided to preserve the crater—both as a scientific research site and as a fascinating tourist attraction that now includes what's supposed to be a pretty good RV park and the sort of carefully contrived visitor center one might find at a real national park.

Erick thought that Meteor Crater might be a great first stop of the day for two reasons. First, even though Meteor Crater was nowhere close to being the world's largest impact crater—that would be the two-hundred-mile-wide Vredefort Crater in South Africa by the way—it was still "the world's best preserved meteor impact site" and therefore an authentic Route 66 superlative, admittedly an obscure one (or maybe they're all obscure). More importantly, Meteor Crater was a spectacular outdoor attraction that could be thoroughly enjoyed by humans and canines alike. Erick envisioned a leisurely forty-five-minute hike around the rim so we could see the crater up close and give Simba a proper walk in the process.

That all sounded good to me. So we took the Meteor Crater Road exit off I-40 and drove seven miles along a picturesque two-lane byway through the high desert. We pulled into the Meteor Crater parking lot, scrambled out of the station wagon, and snapped Simba's leash onto his collar. Then we strolled across the parking lot toward the visitor center where we were met by a discreet little sign that read, "No Pets Allowed."

I was naturally incensed. I mean what possible damage could Simba inflict upon a mile-wide meteor crater that old Daniel Moreau Barringer himself hadn't wreaked during his misbegotten two-decade-long mining effort? I supposed Simba might take a dump on their precious meteor crater. But if he did, I had poop bags at the ready. That being said, I knew from bitter experience that it would likely be useless to reason with whoever was guarding the entrance. So, instead, I decided to evade this petty edict by finding an alternate route to the crater rim.

The only other time I had attempted this particular sort of trespass was in my early thirties at Hearst Castle, on California's Central Coast. Thoroughly disappointed when I pulled into the parking lot only minutes after closing time, my traveling companion and I found an unlocked gate, swung it open and attempted to drive our rental car up the long winding road to press baron William Randolph Hearst's grandiose mish-mash of a house.

I wasn't going to break in or anything. But I'd just driven forty miles out of my way to see this celebrated pile, so I figured I should at least take a quick peek at the exterior and maybe a brief stroll around the formal gardens. Needless to say, I was apprehended well short of my goal—and mercifully released with only a warning. Anyway, I figured Meteor Crater was a much larger target with a much smaller security detail. So it was at least worth a shot.

"Hey, Erick," I said, not too loudly, "I'm going to try to find a way around the visitor center. I'm pretty sure we can get Simba to the crater rim without anyone spotting us."

Erick just shook his head and said, "Okay, do what you have to."

So Simba and I sauntered as nonchalantly as possible around the perimeter of the parking lot. Then I glanced furtively out the front gate searching for a hidden access road or a path that might lead to the main attraction. But needless to say, Barringer Crater Enterprises didn't really want idiots like me ducking their eighteen-dollar admission fee and tramping willy-nilly over their so-called scientific research site. So there were chain-link fences and a high berm—or maybe it was just the crater rim—between the parking lot and the main attraction. And without significantly more local knowledge, it looked as if the only way Erick and I would get anywhere near the meteor crater—or even glimpse it for that matter—was by paying the posted tariff and passing through the visitor center *sans* pooch.[5] Clever, these Barringers!

That, of course, meant that Simba's walk would be limited to a fifteen-minute stroll around the big boring parking lot. And that he would live the rest of his life—however long or short that might be—without ever seeing the world's best-preserved meteor impact site. It also meant that he would be confined to the station wagon with a bowl of water, a hunk of braided rawhide for chewing purposes and an open moon roof while Erick and I ran up for a quick look at the crater. Fortunately, we were now more than a mile above sea level and it was cool enough to leave Simba in the car without fear of heat prostration.

And I have to admit that the visitor center with its huge cantilevered observation decks did afford a magnificent view of the vast crater. It also had two full floors of genuinely informative exhibits about meteors, meteorites, and meteor strikes, not only in the great Southwest but also all around the world. And to pad things out a bit, there were several exhibits about the Apollo space program—including a full-scale reproduction of the Apollo capsule—because NASA astronauts, for apparent reasons, used the crater for training purposes before they blasted off for the moon.

The visitor center's very straightforwardly named Rock Shop had a full range of excellent fossils, which I collected as a boy. So I can tell you these were really good ones. And true to its claim, Me-

---

[5] I have since emailed Brad Andes, president of Meteor Crater Enterprises and a very nice man who adores dogs. I asked him about the security setup at Meteor Crater. To make a long story short, they have remote sensing equipment that alerts a central guardhouse whenever morons like me try to encroach upon nonpublic areas of the crater. So there—you've been warned.

teor Crater itself was very well preserved with almost no evidence of the futile mining operation mounted here a century ago. Naturally, we were disappointed that we couldn't share the first entry on Erick's Wonder List with good old Simba. But fortunately, the next two stops were right up his alley.

In order to fully appreciate the second entry on Erick's Wonder List for the day, you have to be, as they euphemistically say, "of a certain age." Because if you are of that age and you ever hear anyone even casually mention Winslow, Arizona, pretty much the only thing you can think of, no matter how hard you try is, maestro please:

> I was standin' on a corner in Winslow, Arizona
> And such a fine sight to see.

Which are, of course, the first two lines of the second verse of the venerable Eagles anthem, "Take It Easy."

"Take It Easy" was the very first cut on the very first Eagles LP. So it set the tone for what would eventually become one of the best-selling musical acts of all time. It was composed back in 1971 when Eagles front man Glenn Frey lived in a modest first floor apartment in the Echo Park section of Los Angeles directly above singer-songwriter Jackson Browne, who lived in the basement. Again, if you're old enough, you might remember Jackson Browne from his 1977 hit, "Running on Empty" or maybe "Doctor My Eyes," which was a top ten tune in 1972.

So apparently Jackson Browne was sitting at his keyboard day after day trying to compose "Take It Easy." But he always got stuck right after, "and such a fine sight to see." Glenn Frey heard Browne singing the same musical phrase over and over through his floorboards. And eventually he marched downstairs and handed Browne the next few lines of the song, which are, of course:

It's a girl, my Lord, in a flatbed Ford
Slowing down to take a look at me.

Frey's contribution apparently broke the creative logjam and the two front men quickly finished the composition side by side. Then Browne graciously allowed the Eagles to record "Take It Easy" on their eponymous debut album. And the rest, as they say, is rock 'n' roll history.

Why this particular song exerts such a visceral pull on decrepit geezers like Erick and me I cannot tell you. But it does. When I was cruising through this same stretch of northern Arizona with my first wife and three young children back in 1996, I practically insisted on pulling off the interstate and rolling into Winslow just so I could stand on a corner, any corner really, and croon a few verses of "Take It Easy"—much, of course, to my children's dismay. And to this day, when I can barely remember my home phone number or what I ate for lunch, I can still recall every lyric in the song.

Winslow's town fathers decided to cash in on this generational peccadillo. And only a year after I butchered "Take It Easy" on a random Winslow, Arizona, street corner, they acquired their own random corner—West Second Street and North Kinsley Avenue—so they could build Standin' on the Corner Park. (Shouldn't it be Standin' on *a* Corner Park? Oh, well.) Funds were quickly raised, and the little pocket park was completed in less than two years. It now features a brick patio—each brick bearing the name of a donor—a life-size metal statue of a generic 1970s singer-songwriter dude in bell-bottom jeans—meant, I suppose, to be the protagonist of the song—and most prominently, a forty-foot *trompe l'oeil* mural depicting, you guessed it, "a girl, my Lord, in a flatbed Ford slowing down to take a look at me." And if you look at the mural carefully, you'll see an eagle perched on a *trompe l'oeil* windowsill—a richly deserved, though likely unauthorized, nod to the boys in the band.

But here's the really sweet part. Once upon a time, when busy Route 66 ran through the middle of town, Winslow, Arizona, was a popular stopover for bleary motorists shuttling between Chicago and LA. But when the newly constructed Interstate 40 bypassed Winslow in the late 1970s, tourist traffic slowed to a trickle and the town's economy slowly withered.

Standin' on the Corner Park changed all of that. In terms of foot traffic, Winslow isn't Grand Central Station or Disneyland or even what it was fifty years ago. But Erick and I aren't the only old fogies drawn off I-40 by nostalgic yearning. Lots of other duffers come here, too—more than two hundred a day in fact. And some of them drop a few tourist dollars in the process. So if a well-crafted song by Jackson Browne and Glenn Frey didn't restore Winslow to its full former glory, then it certainly stemmed its decline—which kind of gives you faith in the power of popular song.

Simba, of course, was entirely unfamiliar with "Take It Easy," or any of the Eagles' songbook really. But he did recognize a nice place to pee when he saw one. Out of respect for the song, we made that happen on West Second Street itself, rather than the donor bricks. And as you might guess, Erick and I took an inordinate number of cell-phone photos next to the hokey bronze statue of the jeans-clad guitar player and in front of the equally hokey mural of the girl in a flatbed Ford. And we did visit the souvenir shop just across North Kinsley Avenue. And, yes, my friends, we did stand on the now officially designated corner in Winslow, Arizona, and belted out the greater part of "Take it Easy."

And standin' on that corner, artlessly crooning the soundtrack of our youth, Erick and I were transported back to a simpler, freer time in our lives—a time before mortgages, colonoscopies, college tuition payments, alimony, Lipitor, and elderly mothers slowly dying from congestive heart failure. A time when the world was full of promise and anything seemed possible. A time, I thought, when life wasn't so goddamned complicated.

But then I reconsidered the lyrics, and I realized that this entire anthem to just takin' it easy, man, is really about a guy who—in the words of the song itself—has "a world of trouble on his mind"… and four women who want to own him… and two who want to stone him… and the sound of his own wheels driving him crazy— whatever that means.

"Take it Easy," I realized, is about a guy who's pretty stressed out, just trying to calm himself down and hoping that the love of the next pretty girl who drives by will somehow save him. Yeah, well, good luck with that, buddy.

So maybe our youth is only a simpler, freer time in retrospect—just a different set of problems that only seem less perplexing now because we eventually figured out how to solve those problems—or better yet let them go. And maybe twenty years from now, when I'm in my late seventies—if I'm lucky enough to survive that long—I'll look back on my life way back when I was fifty-nine and think, "Wow, those were the good old days—a simpler, freer time when I didn't have to visit the cardiologist every week or wear adult diapers or attend my friends' funerals."

I suppose it's a testament to the human spirit that most of us gaze back upon the serpentine course of our lives and mostly remember the good stuff. I guess that's healthy because people who dwell on old slights and missed opportunities tend to become bitter over time. Still, it probably wouldn't hurt to go one step further and appreciate our lives just as they unfold rather than only in retrospect. Nostalgia for the present! Yeah, that's the ticket! So standin' on a corner in Winslow, Arizona, I resolved to roundly enjoy the here and now—at least, that is, until one of my idiot children wrecks another car or I get a certified letter from the IRS saying they're going to audit my last three returns.

At any rate, I can't imagine how sick and tired the good citizens of Winslow must be, having to listen to aging Baby Boomers like Erick and me butcher the same great song day after day. But they'll just have to deal with it because (a) that song put Winslow back on the map and (b) singing that particular tune in that particular place was a sweet moment for a couple of old guys schlepping a dying dog across America.

Song sung, Erick and I lifted Simba back into the station wagon in the usual manner and resumed our cross-country journey with smiles on our faces and love in our hearts, as happy as Labradors—which, I presume, have a substantially less-developed sense of their own mortality, although it's difficult to know for sure.

If Standin' on the Corner Park hearkened back to an earlier era in our lives, then our next stop, fifty miles further east, evoked a much, much earlier time on planet Earth—the Triassic period of the Mesozoic era to be precise.

So for all of you non-paleontologists out there, the Triassic period was the 50-million-year-long span that immediately preceded the 56-million-year-long Jurassic period, which is familiar to nearly everyone from the wildly popular *Jurassic Park* movie franchise. Or to put it another way, it was between 200 and 250 million years ago in the age of the early dinosaurs.

Back then this stretch of land, now known as the Painted Desert, was a very different place. First of all, it was a low plain, not a mile-high desert plateau. And due to continental drift, it was much closer to the equator—near the southwest shore of Pangaea, the supercontinent that comprised nearly all of Earth's dry land before it eventually broke up into the six continents we know today.

The climate in southern Pangaea was hot and humid. In fact, the entire Earth, on average, was five-and-a-half-degrees Fahrenheit warmer than it is now—even with our justifiably alarming carbon-induced climate change. There were volcanoes to the south and an ocean to the west. And a multitude of rivers and streams flowed lazily across the loamy plains nurturing a rich variety of life.

When it rained, which it did quite often, fallen tree trunks would sometimes wash off the mountains and down into riverbeds where they sank into the primordial ooze. Most of these logs did the usual thing, rotting away over the course of a few decades. But some were so deeply buried in the muck that they were sequestered from the oxygen necessary for decomposition. These logs remained intact. And when water carrying volcanic ash seeped into the sediment, the silica and colorful metallic elements in the ash gradually replaced the organic material in the logs, molecule by molecule, until the fallen tree trunks were wondrously transformed into perfectly log-shaped masses of multicolored quartz crystal.

Some 165 million years later, tectonic forces lifted the low Triassic plain 5,400 feet above sea level. Wind and rain gradually eroded the sedimentary rock laid down in the interim. And that left what Erick, Simba, and I witnessed upon our arrival at Petrified Forest National Park—namely sandstone and siltstone hills, buttes, and mesas gorgeously banded in warm tones of red, ochre, and rust in the ineffably beautiful Painted Desert. And in this section of the

Painted Desert were thousands of fantastical petrified tree trunks strewn haphazardly across the prospect.

Needless to say, large masses of semiprecious stone scattered prolifically across an unprotected plain tend to attract fortune seekers. The first U.S. military surveyors who rode across the Painted Desert in the mid-1850s filled their saddlebags with chunks of petrified wood. And when word of the incredible crystallized logs leaked out, enterprising prospectors flocked to the Painted Desert and hauled them away by the wagonload. In the 1890s, gem collectors dynamited the petrified logs in order to loot chunks of crystal more conveniently. And in 1905, the pioneering environmentalist John Muir gravely informed President Theodore Roosevelt that pillagers were shipping railroad cars full of petrified wood "back East to make jewelry, book ends, table tops, mantel pieces, and curios." For a while, there was even talk of setting up a stone mill here that would grind petrified wood into the sort of grit used in the manufacture of sandpaper. Happily that spectacularly bad idea never gained traction.

It wasn't until 1906—when our most outdoorsy of presidents, Teddy Roosevelt, signed into law the so-called Antiquities Act—that this natural wonder was finally protected as the Petrified Forest National Monument. The national monument became a national park in 1962. And in 2004, the second President Bush more than doubled its size to 341 square miles.

But even though this is now government-protected land, there aren't that many "protection employees" here—sometimes as few as two at a time. So each year, tens of thousand of tourists take advantage of the situation. And perfectly nice folks who wouldn't dream of shoplifting a candy bar from a convenience store or pilfering lumber from a construction site seem entirely at ease grabbing pocketfuls, even the occasional trunk full, of petrified wood and taking it home. There is no way to know exactly how much of the semiprecious stone they take, but one ranger told me that approximately 5 percent of all visitors—so about thirty thousand tourists a year—pilfer at least some. And their annual haul can be measured in tons.

That's the bad news. The good news is that, even after a century and a half of gratuitous looting, there's still an awful lot of petrified wood here—millions of tons, in fact. The other reasonably good news is that remorseful pillagers actually return up to a hundred pounds of petrified wood each month—mostly by mail. Some looters are merely guilt struck. But a surprisingly large number are convinced that their petrified booty precipitated a streak of bad luck that couldn't otherwise be explained. These restituted rocks—which the rangers stack in big piles because they don't know which part of the park they came from—are often accompanied by so-called "conscience letters" that apologize for the larceny.

When Erick, Simba, and I pulled up to the Petrified Forest National Park entrance station and paid the very reasonable ten-dollar admission fee, a friendly Park Service employee handed us a brochure with a map. The map indicated that there were approximately forty miles of paved road running through the preserve, built mostly by Franklin Roosevelt's Civilian Conservation Corps during the Great Depression. And all along these roads were attractions with fairy-tale names like Jasper Forest, Agate Bridge, and Blue Mesa.

Erick and I wanted to see as much of the Petrified Forest as possible. But the brochure also mentioned that the park closed at seven. And, unfortunately, we were a little late to the party.

We had left Las Vegas at eight in the morning. And if we had driven straight through to the Petrified Forest, we would have gotten there at around two in the afternoon. But first the Arizona rainstorm slowed us down. Then we stopped at Meteor Crater and Winslow. And now it was four thirty in the afternoon, which meant that Erick, Simba, and I would have only a couple of hours to explore what promised to be Erick's premier wonder of the day. Luckily, unlike Meteor Crater, the Petrified Forest was only too happy to admit Simba. "Please take your furry friends on trails and even backpacking in the wilderness area," proclaimed the brochure. Now this was my kind of natural wonder.

I have been fortunate enough to view some pretty spectacular vistas over the course of my long life. The Grand Canyon never disappoints. South Africa's Garden Route is a wild medley of scenic surprises. And Big Sur's oceanfront escarpments define the word *dramatic*. But when Erick, Simba, and I pulled into the small parking area at Chinde Point, a few miles past the entrance station, we witnessed a spectacle we'll never forget.

When Erick and I jumped out of the car and helped Simba climb down from the back, we all gazed northward over the Painted Desert and gasped. It was cool and dry where we stood. But off in the distance cumulonimbus clouds—perfectly flat and midnight blue on the bottom, fluffy white on top—were drifting across the high-desert plateau discharging visible sheets of gray rain at a forty-five-degree angle. The landscape was sand-colored in the foreground with brown and gray-banded buttes in the middle and then shockingly beautiful pink, rose, and salmon-colored hills rolling off toward the horizon. Painted Desert, indeed! The one advantage to our last-minute arrival was that the late afternoon light lent the pink hills an otherworldly glow that would have been lost in the midday sun.

"Holy shit," I said to Erick. "This is one of the most beautiful places I've ever seen."

"Yeah, it's pretty spectacular," said Erick, who, unlike me, rarely swears. Also, unlike me, Erick had been here before. And he seemed delighted that I was as entranced with the Painted Desert as he was. Erick, Simba, and I stood at Chinde Point peering out across the vast plain for maybe ten or fifteen minutes before we climbed back into the car to see what else we might find. Since time was short, we rolled past Blue Mesa and Agate Bridge—both now added to my bucket list—so we could spend more time in Jasper Forest, which of course wasn't a forest at all, but rather a forest's worth of crystalline tree trunks strewn across the desert like enormous Pick-up Sticks.

In Jasper Forest, at five thirty in the afternoon, Simba finally got a proper walk in a setting that both delighted and bewildered him. Simba seemed to like the idea of fallen tree trunks lying all over the place. But when he stopped to sniff them, they didn't seem quite right to him. We sometimes forget to what extent dogs rely on their noses to make sense of the world. And these tree-shaped objects that looked like wood but smelled like stone obviously confused him. To Simba, they were probably like those lovely little pieces of plastic sushi you see in the front windows of Japanese restaurants—fun to look at, but a disturbing simulacrum nonetheless.

Erick offered to take a cell-phone photo of Simba and me that would turn out to be one of Simba's last portraits and certainly one of his best. In the photo, Simba and I are standing behind a massive reddish-brown petrified log laid out on the ground. The log, which closely resembles a modern-day redwood tree right down to its stone "bark," is cracked through in a few places but otherwise looks much like it did when it burbled down into the Triassic muck 200 million years ago.

I am looking straight into the camera and smiling, as happy humans do. And Simba is peering out across the landscape and smiling, as happy Labradors do. The flat-bottomed clouds are dark behind us. And they are dark above my head. But directly over Simba is a perfect little hole in the clouds—a small round patch of bright clear blue sky that looks like nothing so much as a portal to heaven.

Erick, Simba, and I reluctantly quit the sublime Petrified Forest at six thirty in the evening. It had been a magnificent sojourn—a balm for the soul and a splendid outdoor adventure—particularly for Simba who had joyously sniffed the high-desert air, savored the sweet breeze in his face, and happily rambled around Jasper Forest—to the extent his arthritis allowed. Along with Meteor Crater and Winslow, Arizona, that made three great stopovers during our second day on the road. So kudos to Erick and his Wonder List!

But now it was time for my own modest contribution to the day's itinerary: the frontier charm of Gallup, New Mexico, and the historic El Rancho Hotel—self-proclaimed "Home of the Movie Stars." When Erick pulled the station wagon back onto I-40, I tapped Google Maps and saw we were only fifty miles from the Arizona–New Mexico border. Gallup was only twenty miles beyond that, and the summer sun wouldn't set until quarter past eight. So we'd definitely make it to Gallup before nightfall. And that was great, because I wanted to see for myself in the clear light of day just how real-life Gallup, New Mexico, stacked up to my romantic Old West vision of it.

When we pulled into Gallup fifty minutes later, I got my first good look at the place. And I could see right away that I would now have to completely rethink my happy-go-lucky policy of visiting random locales merely because I liked the sound of their names. Because in sharp contrast to elegant Spoleto, Italy; bucolic Luang Prabang; and the South Seas paradise of Bora Bora; shabby old Gallup, New Mexico, looked far worse than it sounded. Gallup's retail economy seemed to be founded largely upon its dozens of bars, taverns, and liquor stores, its many Native American craft emporia, and a shockingly large number of pawnbrokers and payday loan shops.

As it turns out, Gallup inherited its lyrical moniker from one David L. Gallup, local paymaster for the short-lived and long-defunct Atlantic and Pacific Railroad. Mr. Gallup established the railroad's regional headquarters here in 1880. And back then, whenever railroad employees wanted to collect their wages they would say, "I'm going to Gallup." When the town was officially founded in 1881, the name stuck.

These days, Gallup's population is more than 40 percent Native American. And it is surrounded on three sides by Indian reservations.[6] The Navajo Reservation, the largest Native American homeland in the United States, is located to the north and west. The smaller Zuni Pueblo is twenty-five miles south. And the Hopi

---

[6] In case you were wondering, both "Native American" and "Indian" are considered politically correct. According to "'American Indian' or 'Native American?'" by Dennis Gaffney, www.pbs.org, April 4, 2006, "A 1995 Census Bureau survey that asked indigenous Americans their preferences... found that 49 percent preferred the term *Indian* and 37 percent *Native American*."

Reservation, a separate enclave within the Navajo nation, is within easy driving distance. So Gallup is sometimes called a "border town," or more grandly, "The Indian Capital of the World."

But it wasn't that long ago that Gallup had some other less flattering nicknames. At least until the late 1980s, it was widely known as "Drunk City" or "Drunk Town, USA." That's because alcohol has been banned on the surrounding Indian reservations since the mid-nineteenth century, but it's always been legal in Gallup. So every weekend, a substantial number of Navajos, Hopis, and Zunis would jump in their pickups and drive into Gallup—often to sell handicrafts and jewelry and then, as often as not, to purchase and consume prodigious quantities of liquor, beer, and fortified wine.

The consequences were predictable. Every weekend brought flagrant displays of public intoxication. Every winter dozens of passed out Indians froze to death in the fields and ravines surrounding Gallup. And a calamitous number of fatal auto accidents occurred when drunken revelers tried to drive themselves home after a big night out. In 1985, the National Institute on Alcoholism and Alcohol Abuse made it official. When it came to heavy drinking, Gallup and surrounding McKinley County lead the nation by a large margin.

Change was a long time coming. But over the course of the 1990s and 2000s, state and local officials gradually addressed Gallup's egregious alcohol problem. They shuttered the town's bustling drunk tank and opened the Na'Nizhoozhi[7] Alcohol Treatment Center. Local law enforcement cracked down on bars and liquor stores

---

[7] Navajo for "Gallup."

that peddled their cut-rate hooch to intoxicated patrons. And they boarded up the entirely-too-convenient drive-up windows at Gallup's copious liquor outlets.

These steps mitigated the problem but didn't really solve it. McKinley County still has the highest alcoholism and cirrhosis rates in New Mexico—a state not noted for its sobriety. Winter still brings an unconscionable number of deaths from exposure. And not everyone is comfortable with a public safety system that empowers generally white "Community Service Aides" to throw generally Native American inebriates into "protective custody." But like I said, it's better than it used to be. And perhaps it was only because we rolled into town on a Tuesday night instead of a weekend, but Erick and I didn't see a single drunk careening along the nearly deserted streets of Gallup.

We did, however, see telltale signs of Gallup's other major affliction, which is, of course, poverty. Because in addition to its alcohol issues, McKinley County has the lowest per capita income in New Mexico. And in 2013, U.S. Census Bureau figures pinpointed Gallup as the second-poorest community in the entire United States.[8] So along with Gallup's ubiquitous pawnbrokers and loan shops, Erick and I couldn't help but notice a few presumably homeless guys looking for a place to bivouac and some reasonably well-dressed folks tramping along the side of the highway who probably would have been driving if they could afford a car. And, oh yeah, Gallup's violent crime rate is five times the national average. But, thankfully, Erick and I didn't experience that scourge either.

---

[8] The poorest town in the United States that year was Lumberton, North Carolina.

Of course, every town has its charms, even Gallup, New Mexico. There are nine or ten beautiful murals in the downtown area that depict local history and various Native American themes. Gallup's tastefully renovated railroad depot houses an impressive cultural center. And of course, you can buy all the decorative silver, turquoise jewelry, woven rugs, and other Indian handicrafts you'll ever need at Gallup's umpteen craft shops and "trading posts."

It's also probably worth noting that in 2013, map and atlas publisher Rand McNally tapped Gallup as "America's Most Patriotic Small Town"—although that distinction may have been largely based on historical considerations such as the brave and effective Navajo code talkers of World War II and Gallup's immensely popular Korean War Congressional Medal of Honor winner, Hiroshi "Hershey" Miyamura.

But honestly, I'm not sure why the nearly 50 percent Native American population of Gallup would feel particularly patriotic. In the mid-1860s, the commander of the Department of New Mexico, General James Henry Carleton, ordered the celebrated frontiersman Kit Carson to wage a scorched-earth campaign against the Navajo nation that effectively destroyed its food supply. Then the astoundingly racist general[9] followed that up with a series of three-hundred-mile death marches to Bosque Redondo, New Mexico, that were collectively dubbed "The Long Walk." Nearly a third of all Navajo men, women, and children perished from starvation and exposure before they were finally allowed to return to their ancestral

---

[9] Carleton's written orders to Carson included the following: "The [Navajo] men are to be slain whenever and wherever they can be found. The women and children may be taken prisoners." politicalquotes.org.

lands in 1868. So Navajos feeling patriotic toward America is sort of like Jews feeling patriotic toward Germany—although at least the Navajos put up a good fight for a while.

Okay, now that I got that off my chest, let's get back to our story. Because smack in the middle of all this alcohol-fueled, poverty-stricken, crime-ridden sadness was—ta-dah!—the El Rancho Hotel, self-proclaimed "Home of the Movie Stars." When Erick and I pulled into the El Rancho's parking lot, we didn't quite know what to make of the place. I had already phoned ahead to make sure that Simba would be welcome here. And whoever took that call made it clear that what I did with my dog was of absolutely no interest to him. So I guessed that was handled.

But the "Home of the Movie Stars" had some other puzzling aspects to it. First of all, there were eight or nine Harley-Davidson motorcycles parked outside, which might or might not indicate that we would be sharing our accommodations not with old-time luminaries of the silver screen but rather with a marauding band of Hell's Angels—or this being the great Southwest, maybe a Bandidos M.C. chapter roaring down the Mother Road. So that might not be good. Secondly, the building itself was a curious mash-up of half-timbered Tudor balconies, a large Georgian portico, and some lumpy Spanish colonial stonework with a bit of ivy-covered stucco thrown in. There was also an impressively large bronze eagle poised to take flight from one of the railings. And there were two somewhat redundant signs hanging over the entrance.

The larger neon sign on top read "Hotel el Rancho." The smaller sign directly beneath it read, "El Rancho Hotel." And then there was a third lit-up sign on the shoulder of Route 66 that read "Hotel & Motel El Rancho." So apparently consistent branding wasn't a corporate priority. Finally, there was another sign above the front door that sported what I took to be the hotel's auxiliary motto (after "Home of the Movie Stars.") It read "Charm of Yesterday… Convenience of Tomorrow." Now that sounded good, at least in theory. But as Erick and I yanked our suitcases out of the backseat and gently offloaded Simba, both claims seemed dubious.

But as it turned out, I was at least half wrong. Because the front doors of the El Rancho Hotel or the Hotel el Rancho or the El Rancho Hotel and Motel or whatever this place was called were, in fact, magical portals to a bygone era. For while the El Rancho's exterior had clearly evolved on an ad hoc basis, its spacious two-story lobby was a lovingly preserved vestige of the hotel's glory years. And yes, my friends, it fairly oozed the charm of yesterday.

Imagine, if you will, a cavernous two-story room with lustrous brown ceramic floor tiles covered here and there with gorgeous Navajo rugs. The white stucco ceiling is supported by dark wooden posts and hand-hewn rafters. And at the far end of the room—which manages to be both impressively large and comfortably cozy at the same time—is a hearth surrounded by pearly white tiles. On either side of the fireplace are two massive semicircular staircases constructed from gray fieldstones, split-log stair treads, and varnished handrails crafted from tree branches. The treads are covered with blood-red carpet runners that lead up to a large open gallery running along three sides of the room. The gallery's exposed brick walls are hung with six-foot-high framed black-and-white photos depicting Navajos in traditional garb. And between these larger prints are dozens of eight-by-ten publicity photos, each inscribed with a heart-felt message from one of the many glamorous movie stars who bunked at the El Rancho back in the day.

The lobby is furnished with sofas and lounge chairs sporting a wagon-wheel motif and brown-and-white cowhide seat cushions that might be considered tacky somewhere else but are right on the money here. Throw in a few mounted deer heads and some stained-glass pendant lights and you've got yourself one heck of a lobby. In fact, you can easily imagine Gary Cooper, Jane Wyman, John Wayne, and maybe Rosalind Russell lounging around this gorgeous old-school lobby languidly puffing their Lucky Strikes and sipping Rob Roys from lowball glasses. And apparently every one of those stars and quite a few others actually did that—or something very similar.

After admiring the lobby for a few minutes, Erick and I mo-seyed over to the check-in desk, which was manned by a short, slight, middle-aged man who looked as if he might have lived life pretty hard at some point.

"Good evening," I said, "My name is Cohen, and I reserved two rooms for this evening."

"What kinda rooms ya want?" the desk clerk asked.

Hmmm. I thought I'd settled that when I made the reservation.

"It doesn't really matter," I replied. "We're only stayin' over fer one night, so any a' yer single rooms'll do just fine."

Crap! I was unconsciously mimicking his New Mexico accent, which is a truly annoying habit of mine. Fortunately, the desk clerk didn't seem to notice. He pulled out a laminated rate card and said, "Okay, we got singles for $109. And if you got triple-A, then it's $98 plus tax."

"That's fine," I said using my everyday non-New Mexico accent. "And, yes, I do have triple-A. Do you take American Express?" (Ever since Laureen landed her new job, I have endeavored to be loyal to her employer.)

The check-in clerk ran my card and then said to Erick, "Okay, you got the Katharine Hepburn room. And you," he said turning to me, "got the Betty Hutton." Then he handed us two old-fashioned brass keys—not the plastic keycards you usually get these days.

"Does that mean Katharine Hepburn actually stayed in Erick's room?" I asked with boyish enthusiasm. I instantly knew it was a stupid question. The check-in clerk confirmed that with a sideways glance and didn't bother to respond.

"Okay, then," I continued. "Where would we find the elevator?"

"Stairs over there," he said, pointing at the massive semicircular staircases.

"Do you happen to have an elevator?" I asked. "We have these big rolling suitcases, and old Simba here has arthritis. So he has trouble with stairs." Simba, hearing his name, smiled and panted in agreement.

"Yup," he said, and without another extraneous word, he stepped out from behind the counter and led us to an ancient manually operated elevator. So much for "The Convenience of Tomorrow." The elevator slowly creaked its way up to the second floor. And when it shuddered to a stop, the desk clerk/elevator operator opened the door and pointed down a long and narrow, dimly-lit corridor with compact fluorescent bulbs, exposed water pipes, and assorted electrical wires running along its ceiling.

As Erick, Simba, and I made our way down the shadowy hallway, I squinted to read the names of the movie stars printed on little plaques mounted to each guest room door. I'm sort of a classic film buff. So most of the names—like Errol Flynn, Jean Harlow, and Joseph Cotten—were entirely familiar. A few others—like Jack Oakie and Irene Manning—were a bit more obscure. But eventually we found a door marked Katherine Hepburn where we dropped off Erick. Then Simba and I proceeded to the Betty Hutton Room.

Betty Hutton, *nee* Elizabeth June Thornburg of Battle Creek, Michigan, is probably best known for replacing a very uncooperative Judy Garland in the role of Annie Oakley in the 1950 film version of *Annie Get Your Gun*. But she also played the wonderfully zany Trudy Kockenlocker in one of my favorite films of all time, the 1944 Preston Sturges satire, *The Miracle of Morgan's Creek*. The preternaturally perky Ms. Hutton was actually Paramount Pictures' top female box-office draw for a ten-year span beginning in the early 1940s. And despite the fact that she was young, beautiful, prodigiously talented, and globally famous for a time, Betty Hutton was not one of your snooty Hollywood prima donnas—not if she was willing to stay in this room.

I do realize that I had specifically requested a bargain-rate $98 single, but the Betty Hutton Room was small, very small—so small, in fact, that when I pulled the bedspread off the double bed, folded it in four, and laid it over the well-worn carpet to make a bed for

Simba, there wasn't much left in the way of useable floor space. And the bathroom was even smaller, like something you might find on a boat or an airplane. It did have a pint-sized shower. But, by all appearances, neither the bathroom nor the room itself had been updated since… well, maybe since Betty Hutton stayed here in the 1950s.

But, honestly, none of that really mattered because (a) Simba was all about coziness when he slept—which was most of the time these days—and (b) we were only staying one night. Plus the El Rancho's fabulous lobby and nostalgic photo gallery more than compensated for any shortcomings in our room.

Before I changed for dinner, I called my dad to find out how my mother was holding up. Long story short, she wasn't holding up well.

"Did something specific happen?" I asked.

"Well, first we went to Dr. Kross's office, and he said that even with the oxygen concentrator running twenty-four hours a day, her blood oxygen level is way too low."

"Do you know why it's getting worse?" I asked.

"It's the same thing that's been happening for the last two years," he said. "Only now it's speeding up. Basically her heart has gotten to the point where it can't clear enough fluid from her lungs for the air to get it. So, in effect, she's drowning."

"Does it help to turn the oxygen up?" I asked (as if he wouldn't think of that).

"It's already up to eight," my dad replied, "and it only goes to ten. So we don't have a lot of headroom here. Also, last night she tried to get up at three a.m. to go the bathroom, and she didn't use her walker, so she fell on the floor. And normally I would have called your brother to come over and help me lift her up, but he's out of town this week, so I had to call 911. They were very nice and all, but I was kind of embarrassed that I couldn't get her back into bed on my own."

Oh Christ! I thought. This was getting much worse, much faster than I expected. But there wasn't much I could do at the moment because I was in frickin' Gallup, New Mexico.

"Well, hang in there," I said to my dad. "For what it's worth, I should be in Pittsburgh in about three days. I'm not exactly sure what I can do to help you, but I'll do whatever you want."

"You're already doing something," said my father, who always put the best possible spin on everything I had ever done in my life, even when it wasn't entirely warranted. "Your mother's very excited to see you. And I know it sounds crazy, but when she has something like that to look forward to, it really keeps her going. In fact it's all she's been talking about for the last week."

"Okay, thanks Dad," I said. "I love you."

I lay back on the bed and tried to sort out my priorities, "Okay," I thought, "Simba's slowly dying—at least I hope it's slowly—and I need to get him to New York to see Laureen and the girls as soon as possible. And my mother is slowly dying, and I need to get myself to Pittsburgh to see her as soon as possible. Simba can only take so many hours a day in the car. So we can't go much faster. I guess we just need to keep pushing forward."

I got up from the bed and squeezed into the micro-bathroom to wash my face and brush my teeth. I called Erick on his cell phone to see if he was ready for dinner. And then to avoid a replay of the whole Venetian Hotel Panic Incident, I brought Simba down to the car with me so he could sleep in the back of the station wagon while Erick and I ate.

Once we were in the car, I found a four-star restaurant on Trip-Advisor. (The local Taco Bell had been awarded five stars by the way.) I dropped the address into Google Maps. Then we set forth to find it. We followed Google's step-by-step directions to a modest residential neighborhood with no streetlights. Then we circled around in the car for a while before concluding that either Google was wrong or, more likely, that the restaurant had ceased to exist. So we admitted defeat and headed back to the El Rancho, which had its own small-but-charming restaurant just off the lobby.

Erick and I scarfed down some decent Mexican food. And, honestly, it was nice having Simba right upstairs where I could check up on him any time I wanted. It was also nice bedding down with my old buddy in such tight quarters—especially after the very unsettling conversation with my father. Thanks to Simba and his soft rhythmic snoring, I managed to sleep straight through the night entirely undisturbed by carousing Navajos, imaginary motorcycle gangs, or the restless shade of Betty Hutton, whose three estranged daughters skipped their own mother's funeral. But that's another story.

12. JUNKYARD DOG

Simba was now our virtual alarm clock, always set for dawn. So we were able to wake up, pack our bags, take the old dog for a sunrise stroll, and still decamp from the El Rancho well before the stroke of seven. Then Erick and I pulled onto Route 66 and began an earnest search for a decent cup of coffee. Less than a half mile down the road, we spotted a little, white clapboard shed with neat red trim and a black-and-white sign that read Blunt Brothers Coffee.

"What do you think?" asked Erick.

"I'm not sure we have a lot of options," I replied.

"Okay. Then let's do it."

We pulled up to the drive-in window and read the bill of fare, which was posted on a chalkboard hanging from the side of the shed. Blunt Brothers' hot beverage menu was unexpectedly comprehensive, including everything from espresso, chai tea, and organic macchiatos to a "coconut and macadamia mocha," whatever that was. Being the elitist San Francisco jerks we are, Erick and I both ordered cappuccinos—often a dubious choice in a town this small. But as I keep learning every day, you don't know what you don't know. The cheerful young guy manning the drive-in window turned out to be a master of his craft. And the two sublimely brewed beverages he tendered put Starbuck's, maybe even Peet's, to shame.

"Wow," I said after my first hot foamy sip. "This is a damn good cappuccino." Erick concurred. And with that, shabby old Gallup, New Mexico—which may have had a lot of other problems but still served a magnificent cup of joe—rose a notch in our estimation.

Amarillo, Texas, our ultimate destination that day, was another relatively short hop—only six hours and 424 miles due east. And in Erick's considered opinion, there weren't that many points of interest worth visiting on the barren New Mexico plains or the flat, nearly treeless Texas Panhandle. There were some vaguely famous ice caves about an hour east of Gallup. But ever since I was knocked for a loop by heart-pounding claustrophobia deep inside the Roman catacombs, I've generally tried to avoid caverns, caves, and other subterranean burrows. And ice caves, at least to me, seemed like the worst possible type of subterranean burrow.

Unfortunately, when I vetoed the ice caves for valid psychological reasons, that left only one other entry on Erick's Wonder List for the day, which is probably why he was so darn dramatic about it. As we drove eastward on I-40 all morning, losing three thousand feet in altitude and gaining thirty degrees in temperature, I periodically asked Erick what was on the agenda. But of course, he wouldn't tell me. He just smiled and said, "Wait for it. You'll see."

But then we drove more than 400 miles, stopping only once for gas and dog-pooping purposes, and Erick still hadn't gotten that telltale twinkle in eye.

"Hey, Erick," I finally said. "We're only ten miles from Amarillo, and we haven't seen any wonders of the day yet. What gives?"

"Be patient," he said. "We're almost there."

Another five minutes passed, and I saw an exit sign for Arnot Road coming up on the right.

"Okay," said Erick. "We're here. Take this exit. Then turn left."

After a short drive along the frontage road, we rolled to a stop behind a long line of vehicles improbably parked next to a very large cow pasture. Entire families were clambering out of their cars and squeezing sideways through a narrow gap in the livestock fence. And some of the visitors, mostly kids and teenagers, were rattling cans of spray paint as they gamboled into the field.

At first I couldn't imagine why all these people would make a pilgrimage to a nondescript Texas Panhandle cow pasture or why on Earth they would bring spray paint. But then I saw it. Two or three hundred yards from the road was a long row of ancient graffiti-covered automobiles half-buried nose first in the earth. Erick smiled broadly, proud to present yet another wacky Route 66 oddity.

Without sufficiently considering Erick's sensibilities in the matter, I quickly blurted out, "Hey, I know what this is. It's Cadillac Ranch!"

And Erick said, with a touch of dejection, "Oh, okay, so you already know about this. I thought it would be a surprise."

"No, no, Erick," I replied, "this is great. The only reason I know about Cadillac Ranch is that I had this amazing history of art teacher named Vincent Scully who talked about it in class and showed us a bunch of slides. But, honestly, I didn't remember where it was. And I've always wanted to see it. So this is actually a great surprise. Plus, look. People are bringing their dogs in there."

That seemed to make Erick feel better. So we all climbed out of the car and shimmied through a narrow cattle stile that had no Cadillac Ranch sign, no ticket taker, no posted rules or regulations of any kind, nor any other indication that the general public was in any way welcome here. But since there were already fifty or sixty art enthusiasts milling around the half-buried cars, it seemed like it would be okay to join them.

So, if like most people, you didn't take Vincent Scully's history of art class and don't live in the Texas Panhandle, here's the scoop: Cadillac Ranch consists of ten ancient Cadillacs, each from a different model year between 1949 and 1963. These vehicles are buried nose-first from the front bumper to the top of the windshield at a 51.5-degree angle—supposedly the same angle as the four sides of the Great Pyramid of Giza, but who knows if that's true. And that leaves the passenger compartments and trunks—and since they're vintage Cadillacs, tailfins of various shapes and sizes—proudly protruding into the azure Texas sky. Cadillac Ranch was created in 1974, originally in another cow pasture a few miles away. And it has somehow defied the vicissitudes of time and taste to become an enduring, if somewhat eccentric, classic.

So who would do such a thing? And why? And who would be crazy enough to pay for it? Well, like so many trippy 1970s concoctions, Cadillac Ranch was originally dreamt up in the San Francisco Bay Area. Back then Chip Lord, a recent Tulane School of Architecture graduate; Doug Michels, a Yale architecture grad; and Hudson Marquez, another Big Easy transplant with a Tulane art degree, formed what they termed "a radical art and design collective." At first the trio didn't know what to call their new enterprise. But when they told a friend they wanted to do "underground architecture," the friend, who was likely high at the time, replied, "Oh, you mean like ants?" So they dubbed their new venture Ant Farm.

One day, Marquez, the graphic artist of the group, was sitting with Chip Lord in a rustic NorCal tavern in the Marin County hills. There, Marquez found a kids' book, entitled *The Look of Cars,* sitting on the bar. As he thumbed through the book, he noticed a series of drawings that documented the rise and fall of Cadillac tail fins during the nineteen fifties and sixties. Marquez had a straight up 'Eureka' moment, and on the spot, he sketched out his idea for Cadillac Ranch.

Then, armed with Marquez's zany zeitgeisty concept, the Ant Farm guys set out to find a patron with enough cash and whimsy to purchase and half-bury ten old Cadillacs—and ideally, a spacious patch of land where they could do that. Enter eccentric former banker, local Amarillo TV mogul, and oil heir Stanley Marsh 3.

(Marsh told people—unconvincingly, I think—that he used "3" not "III," because he considered Roman numerals pretentious.)

The Ant Farm guys sent Marsh a plaintive letter requesting funds for their outré scheme. And on March 8, 1974, Marsh wrote back saying he would give them an answer on April Fools' Day, since "it's such an irrelevant and silly proposition that I want to give it all my time and attention." Marsh apparently concluded that Cadillac Ranch was just irrelevant and silly enough, because he put up the requisite cash and lent Ant Farm one of his Amarillo-area cow pastures. Upon hearing the happy news, the Ant Farm guys scoured the great state of Texas for used Cadillacs. And they very quickly—by the end of the year in fact—completed their installation.

So if you think about it, Cadillac Ranch was a pretty arbitrary, spur of the moment conceit—literally back-of-the-napkin stuff. But forty years on, it's still considered the defining artistic achievement of everyone involved. Cadillac Ranch is mentioned in the very first sentence of Stanley Marsh 3's 2014 *New York Times* obituary—prior to several other fascinating tidbits about his life, including the fact that he kept a pet lion and erected dozens of whimsical street signs around Amarillo (e.g. "Road Does Not End"). Also that he secured a coveted spot on President Richard Nixon's infamous "Enemies List" when he wrote Tricky Dick a letter offering to display one of Pat Nixon's Sunday bonnets in a proposed "Museum of Decadent Art." Cadillac Ranch is also mentioned before the far-less-amusing fact that Marsh's "reputation was badly tarnished by accusations that he had sexually abused teenage boys." Lots of teenage boys, actually, but let's stick to the art here.

When asked what Cadillac Ranch meant to him, what its significance was, Marsh replied, somewhat high-mindedly, that it was "a monument to the American dream." And then somewhat less high-mindedly that to him Cadillacs represented money, sex, and "getting away from home for the first time."

The Ant Farm trio was less forthcoming in its exegesis, preferring to let the art speak for itself. Or as Hudson Marquez very plainly put it in a 2013 *LA Weekly* interview, "Anybody who talks about their own art is full of shit."

Ant Farm's 1975 follow-up project, "Media Burn," was significantly less subtle in its semiotics. That short-lived performance piece consisted of two guys dressed as crash-test dummies ramming a tricked-out '59 Cadillac El Dorado Biarritz through a twelve-foot-high pyramid of flaming television sets. Ant Farm mounted this "media event"—it was a new term back then—on the Fourth of July in the parking lot of the Cow Palace, a venerable San Francisco event center that had hosted the 1956 and 1964 Republican National Conventions. And they mischievously invited every television news director in Northern California to send a reporter and camera crew.

The reporters knew, of course, that they, themselves, were the butt of this high-concept joke. But they had to cover it anyway because an enormous white Caddie plowing through a pyramid of flaming televisions is practically the definition of must-see TV. Even Nudie Cohn, the Ukrainian shlockmeister who tricked out Buck Owens' wall-mounted Grande Ville back in Bakersfield, never did anything that flamboyant with a Cadillac.

When Erick, Simba, and I finally made our way out to the ninety-foot-long row of half-buried cars, we could see that they were slowly rusting away and that every square inch of every vehicle was covered in graffiti. Visitors aren't normally encouraged to deface semifamous monumental sculptures. I'm sure Christo or Richard Serra wouldn't appreciate it. But given their distinctly antiestablishment bent, I feel certain the Ant Farm guys wouldn't object. Chip Lord did have all ten Cadillacs repainted matte black when his old friend and partner Doug Michels died in a hiking accident in 2003. But then he let them revert to their natural graffiti-covered state.

Out in the middle of a Texas cow pasture, our fellow art lovers were not only vandalizing the rusty old Caddies, they were also clambering all over them with little regard for their fragile condition. So while this droll monument to the futility of the American Dream or the freedom of the open road or maybe just absurdity for absurdity's sake had survived forty years, it didn't look as if it would last forty more. So Erick and I memorialized this moment in art history with a raft of cell-phone photos that all featured our old buddy Simba lying in the dusty foreground. And for the first time since we left Tiburon, Simba had the opportunity to meet and greet fellow dogs from the Lone Star State and all around this great nation, and to ceremoniously sniff their butts in the shadow of arguably important art.

After an hour or so, we all climbed back into the station wagon. And with a little help from the TripAdvisor app, we were lucky enough to find Tyler's, a terrific little barbecue joint on the outskirts of Amarillo. Happily, Tyler's had two outdoor picnic tables, so Simba was able to join our luncheon. And over heaping plates of top-notch ribs and brisket, Erick and I decided to push past Amarillo and drive another four hours to Oklahoma City, where Simba would suffer his first major health setback of the journey.

About halfway between Amarillo and Oklahoma City, about ten miles over the Texas–Oklahoma border, Erick wanted to pull off the interstate again, so he could make a childhood dream come true. Apparently, when Erick was a lad of seven or eight, back in Norfolk, Virginia, he kept an atlas in his room. And from that atlas, he learned that there was only one municipality, large or small, in the entire U.S. of A. named Erick with a *k*.[10] And that municipality, my friends, was Erick, Oklahoma, pop. 1,052. And guess what? Despite the fact that Erick had lived in six or seven different states over the course of his life—and at one point or another, had visited nearly all the others—he never quite made it to Erick, Oklahoma. And he had always wanted to see it. So now, in his sixty-third year, he would finally get that opportunity.

---

[10] On the United States Board on Geographic Names website (http://geonames.usgs. gov) I found a tiny hamlet in Wheeler County, Georgia, that is also named Erick. It even has an Erick Road and an Erick Church—but please don't tell our Erick about it, because first of all, it would take the blush off Erick, Oklahoma, and secondly, I have no strong desire to visit Wheeler County, Georgia.

So we pulled off I-40 again at the North Sheb Wooley Avenue exit. And lo and behold, the very first thing we saw was pretty much the best thing we could have seen—at least for Erick's purposes. It was a big billboard set low to the ground. And it featured an energetic illustration of a cherry-red 1957 Chevy roaring out of a sunset—or maybe a sunrise—its headlights blazing and some retro Route 66-style type that read, "Welcome to Erick, Oklahoma." It looked like a giant postcard, and it was the perfect backdrop for a photo op. So out came the cell phones.

First I shot Erick, arms akimbo, in front of the Erick sign, then Erick and Simba in front of the Erick sign from a low angle, then Erick giving the thumbs up in front of the Erick sign, then Erick crossing his arms and leaning back in front of the Erick sign—click, click, and done. Then we hopped back into the station wagon and drove a mile or so south on Sheb Wooley Avenue toward Erick, Oklahoma's tiny business district to see how things were going there. And to me, at least, it didn't look as if things were going all that well.

Like Winslow, Arizona, the hamlet of Erick, Oklahoma, sits astride the old Route 66. Also like Winslow, it has legitimate musical roots—probably more legit than Winslow. Because while tiny Erick, Oklahoma, isn't mentioned in any classic rock lyrics I know of, it is the childhood home of the prodigiously talented country-western songsmith, the "King of the Road" himself, Roger Miller. A consummate entertainer, Miller snagged six Grammies on a single, luminous night back in 1966—still the biggest sweep ever for a country-western artist. Then, two decades later, he won a Tony award for scoring the folksy Broadway smash *Big River*, a toe-tapping musical version of *Huckleberry Finn*.

Miller, a lifelong smoker, died from lung and throat cancer at age fifty-six. And these days, Erick honors its favorite son with a homey little Roger Miller Museum at the corner of Roger Miller Boulevard and Sheb Wooley Avenue. Erick also hosts a Roger Miller Festival every October. The festival features three or four concerts, a "King of the Road Classic Car Contest," that apparently pits Oklahoma against Texas, a Little-Miss-type beauty pageant, and in more recent years, a wild hog hunt.

And if that weren't enough celebrity cred for one tiny dot on the map, Erick is also the birthplace of actor-singer-songwriter Sheb Wooley—hence, Sheb Wooley Avenue. I know that right now you're probably asking yourself, "Who the hell is Sheb Wooley?" And honestly, I didn't remember myself until Erick reminded me that he played Pete Nolan opposite Clint Eastwood's Rowdy Yates on the classic 1960s TV series *Rawhide*. And perhaps more importantly, he topped the charts in 1958 with his ubiquitous novelty hit, "The Purple People Eater," which pretty much everyone has heard at some point in their lives. (Oh, come on, you remember: "It was a one-eyed, one-horned, flying purple people eater.") "The Purple People Eater," is either a canny allegory about the vagaries of rock 'n' roll stardom or just an incredibly stupid song. But either way, it's pretty darn catchy. Plus Sheb Wooley taught Roger Miller, his wife's young cousin, how to strum a gee-tar in the first place, so he deserves some credit for that.

But like I said, Erick, Oklahoma, didn't look as if it was particularly thriving in the post-Route-66 era. There seemed to be a few empty storefronts and a couple of marginal enterprises like second-hand stores that tend to pop up when rents drop sufficiently. And, of course, there wasn't much in the way of foot traffic—or really any traffic for that matter.

But looks can be deceiving, particularly to a big-city slicker like me, because I later learned that in 2014, Erick, Oklahoma, boasted an unemployment rate of 2.2 percent, which is pretty much no unemployment at all. And according to a website called "Sperling's Best Places," which apparently tracks such things, Erick's median home price is a spectacularly affordable $64,200, which, if you live in San Francisco or New York, seems practically incredible.

So if you've ever thought about making your home, home on the range, you might want to take a hard look at Erick, Oklahoma, where you can live pretty well very cheaply. And you can definitely get a job there. And every October, you can take in the Roger Miller Festival, show off your classic car, and chow down on some wild hog, which, if you've never had the pleasure, is like the tastiest *treif*[11] ever.

But for the time being at least, I was personally committed to wildly overcrowded, wildly overpriced, wild-hog-free Manhattan. And, unfortunately for Erick and me, the Roger Miller Museum was closed on Tuesdays. So we made a U-turn on Sheb Wooley Avenue and bid Erick, Oklahoma, a fond farewell. And with Erick's fifty-five-year-old dream finally realized, we hopped back onto I-40 and headed east toward Oklahoma City.

---

[11] Yiddish for nonkosher food.

I had been to Oklahoma City only once before—in 1995—and that was under difficult circumstances. Two months prior to my visit—on April 19, 1995, at 9:02 a.m. to be precise—a disgruntled First Gulf War veteran, Special Forces washout, and right-wing sociopath named Timothy McVeigh exacted his revenge on the federal government by bombing the Alfred P. Murrah Federal Building in downtown Oklahoma City. Twenty-six-year-old McVeigh rented a yellow Ryder truck, packed it with nearly three tons of ammonium nitrate fertilizer, nitro-methane fuel, and 500 blasting caps. Then he parked it in front of the Murrah Building, lit a two-minute fuse, popped in his earplugs, and walked away.

The massive explosion ripped the entire north wall off the nine-story federal building, damaged or destroyed 347 other downtown structures, and killed 168 innocent people, including nineteen babies and toddlers just starting their day at the America's Kids Day Care Center on the Murrah building's second floor. McVeigh, who apparently learned some self-serving jargon in the military, later characterized the dead babies and toddlers as "collateral damage," so not worthy of his remorse.

So what exactly was Timothy McVeigh avenging? And why did he target the Murrah building on April 19?

Well, McVeigh, who claims to have been bullied as a child, became convinced over time that the federal government was "the ultimate bully." And as proof of that conviction, he pointed to a disastrous 1993 raid mounted by the Bureau of Alcohol, Tobacco and Firearms in concert with the FBI and, eventually, several other federal and state agencies. What's now called "the Waco Siege" or "the Branch Davidian Massacre," began as a fairly straightforward incursion designed to confiscate a cache of weapons hoarded by an end-of-days religious sect called the Branch Davidians. But when the ATF breached the sect's Mount Carmel compound, the Davidians opened fire, slaying four agents and wounding sixteen others. The agents shot back killing six cult members before they ran low on ammo and retreated.

Then, what was supposed to be a quick in-and-out sortie devolved into a fifty-day nationally televised siege. On the fifty-first day, April 19, 1993, the feds finally lost patience with cult leader David Koresh. And with the reluctant blessing of Bill Clinton's rookie attorney general, Janet Reno, they massed more than 800 law enforcement personnel for a final showdown—a scenario that played right into the Davidians' apocalyptic worldview.

Armed with nine Bradley Fighting Vehicles and five M728 Combat Engineering Vehicles—basically Patton Battle Tanks with bulldozer blades and booms—the feds pierced several buildings in the compound and filled them with tear gas. Then, when the Branch Davidian men, women, and children didn't stream out as expected, they mounted a massive frontal assault.

A fire started—almost certainly set by the Davidians—and it quickly became an inferno. Four hours later, the compound was more or less leveled, and seventy-five more cult members, including nineteen children under the age of six, lay dead in the ashes. Although exactly who killed them—the feds, the Branch Davidians, or both—still remains a matter of controversy.

By nearly anyone's reckoning, the ATF and FBI botched the Waco raid with horrific results. But for the militant antigovernment crowd, the incident had deeper meaning. Along with another bungled raid in Idaho called the Ruby Ridge Incident, the Branch Davidian Massacre confirmed their worst fears. Namely, that the Second Amendment was under federal attack and the century-old doctrine of *posse comitatus*—which prohibits the federal government from using the army against its own citizens—was now a thing of the past.[12] Not one to abide that sort of tyranny, Timothy McVeigh "decided to send a message to a government that was becoming increasingly hostile."

McVeigh got the specific idea to bomb a federal building housing law enforcement agencies from a wildly anti-Semitic, virulently racist novel called *The Turner Diaries.* A perennial bestseller in white supremacist circles from sea to shining sea, *The Turner Diaries* was penned under the pseudonym Andrew Macdonald in 1978. But lurking behind that nom de plume was one William Luther Pierce, III, a former Oregon State physics professor and grand poobah of a now blessedly defunct neo-Nazi network called the National Alliance. Dr. Pierce's lurid race-war fantasy breathlessly imagines America—and eventually the world—as a white Protestant utopia where all the cunning Jews get their just desserts, "inferior races" such

---

[12] The Posse Comitatus Act of 1878—updated in 1956 and 1981—prohibits the federal government from deploying either the Army or the Air Force (which was once part of the Army) domestically. The Navy and Marines are not bound by posse comitatus, but have parallel internal regulations. The National Guard, on the other hand, acts under the authority of individual states and is often used in domestic conflicts.

as "black cannibals" and "repulsive mongrel Puerto Ricans" are either massacred or deported, and every man, woman, and child in sub-Saharan Africa is annihilated—to name just a few of the more loathsome plot points.

But one section of *The Turner Diaries* particularly spoke to young Timothy McVeigh. After the Jewish-controlled U.S. Congress passes the insidious Cohen Act (hey!), federal agents and their black radical henchmen fan out across America in an effort to seize all privately owned firearms—like the ATF did in Waco. And in response, the novel's protagonist, Earl Turner, sparks a glorious whitefolks revolt by blasting FBI headquarters in Washington with—you guessed it—three tons of ammonium nitrate fertilizer packed into a truck.

So basically, Timothy McVeigh took a page from *The Turner Diaries*—the part where Turner and his band of not-so-merry men build and detonate their truck bomb. And on the second anniversary of the Branch Davidian Massacre, he emulated his fictional hero right down to the type, size, and delivery method of the explosive.

In this case, "take a page" is not a figure of speech. When Charlie Hanger, an on-the-ball Oklahoma state trooper, pulled over McVeigh's yellow Mercury sedan less than two hours after the blast, he spotted a manila envelope on the front seat. And inside that envelope were seven photocopied pages from *The Turner Diaries*, which McVeigh employed both as a how-to manual and a message.

Timothy McVeigh died what he hoped would be a martyr's death at the Federal Correctional Complex in Terre Haute, Indiana, on June 11, 2001—the first federal execution in nearly four decades.

Since his vile act had failed to incite a *Turner Diaries*-type white people uprising, McVeigh wanted his execution to be nationally televised thinking that might do the trick. But the federal court would approve only a closed-circuit feed to the victims' families. And that wasn't what you'd call a sympathetic audience.

At the time, the Oklahoma City bombing was the deadliest act of terrorism committed on U.S. soil. But McVeigh's grisly record wouldn't stand for long. Three months to the day after McVeigh's execution, the grim Saudi barbarian Osama bin Laden significantly upped the ante.

But what does all that have to do with my 1995 visit to Oklahoma City? Well, like most people, I was repulsed to the core by both the carnage and its inspiration. And I wanted to do something to help. So since my occupation was creating photo books, I decided to publish a slim volume that documented the heinous event and donate the proceeds to a scholarship fund set up for the 219 children who lost one or both of their parents in the blast. I did something similar to benefit migrant farm workers who lost their housing in the 1989 San Francisco earthquake so I knew it would work.

With so-called "instant books" or "disaster books"—that's what publishers call them—the key to success is getting the product onto bookstore shelves as quickly as possible. Basically, you have a week or so to gather and edit the photos, design the book, and write the captions, then another week to get the book printed and ten days to distribute it. Not long after that, the gruesome event fades in the public mind and sales dry up. So if I wanted to raise as much money as possible for the scholarship fund, I had to get the book out quickly. And as a result, I spent fifteen or sixteen hours a day for six days straight poring over thousands of grisly slides with a magnifying loupe—this was pre-digital—trying to make sure the pictures we used were well-framed, well-composed, and sharply focused.

There is, of course, a world of difference between experiencing a large-scale disaster firsthand and perusing photos of that disaster a few days later. I know, because I've done both. But up to that point in my career, nearly all my books had been lighthearted celebrations of everyday life as it's lived in various countries around the world. So I wasn't mentally prepared to examine thousand of photos of bloody corpses, the dazed faces of devastated family members, exhausted soot-caked first responders, and, worst of all, the slaughtered babies and children.

And traveling to Oklahoma City to launch the book several weeks later brought all of those disturbing images to life. First of all, I arrived in the middle of that crazy lightening storm with 110-mile-per-hour winds that I described to Erick back in Arizona. Then I was privileged to meet some of the heroic first responders and incredibly decent people of Oklahoma City who lost family and friends in the blast. Those encounters took all of those thousands of photos I edited right out of the sphere of dispassionate photojournalism into a far more personal realm.

So the upshot was this: as we drove across the prairie from tiny Erick, Oklahoma, to Oklahoma City on a sunny Tuesday afternoon, I thought it would be a great idea to visit the Oklahoma City National Memorial, which opened its doors five years after my little book was published. And since much of the memorial is outdoors, I hoped Simba might be able to accompany us. But when we actually reached OKC and I began to recognize some of the landmarks I had seen in the photos, the stomach-churning revulsion I felt back in 1995 resurfaced. And I decided to put off the visit, at least for the time being. So I told Erick I was sorry, but I didn't want to see the memorial quite yet—and I do realize that "quite yet" in this case was two full decades after the event.

But, hey, don't get me wrong. By all accounts the Oklahoma City National Memorial is one of the most beautiful, dignified, and tasteful monuments on Earth. It has a graceful block-long reflecting pool bounded at both ends by thirty-foot-high rectangular bronze arches called "the Gates of Time." One arch is inscribed "9:01," the minute before the blast; the other, "9:03," the minute after. And it is a refined and thoughtful representation of the tragedy. And next to the reflecting pool are 168 oversized empty chairs—one for each victim. There is also a lone elm, called "the Survivor Tree," that miraculously withstood the blast and then surprised everyone by sprouting hopeful green buds the following spring. And everyone says that the on-site museum is both informative and moving. But I'm telling you all of this as someone who hasn't seen any of these things. I've only seen them the same way I saw the incident itself—through photographs and videos.

So even though I knew I should visit the Oklahoma City National Memorial, I didn't. And honestly, I felt guilty about that. But it is a measure of Erick's discretion as a stand-up guy on a road trip that when I said I didn't want to go and didn't offer any explanation, he didn't try to discuss it with me or even ask why. He just shrugged and said, "Okay. If that's what you want." And that reminded me what a discerning friend he was.

Huzzah! The dog in the hotel problem has been solved! After making ten freakin' phone calls to find one lousy place in Las Vegas that would admit Simba as a guest, then more or less lucking out at the loosey-goosey El Rancho, I finally stumbled upon a nationwide chain of relatively inexpensive hotels that seemed to welcome canine companions—regardless of weight—at most of its two-thousand-plus locations (or at least the ones we needed.) So, thank you, Hampton Inns by Hilton. And thank you Hampton Inn & Suites Oklahoma City-Bricktown.

After pulling up in front of the hotel, Erick and I took Simba for a brief stroll. Then we checked into our rooms. And since Simba had successfully braved two consecutive dinners, more or less solo, I figured it would probably be okay to let him veg out in front of *Wheel of Fortune* while Erick and I ventured out to find some dinner.

I bid Simba adieu while he was still crunching his kibble. Then Erick and I took off on foot down East Sheridan Avenue. When we hit North Mickey Mantle Drive—the Yankees slugger was a proud

Sooner—we happened upon Nonna's Euro-American Ristorante and Bar, which looked as if it might be a pretty good place to eat. And it was. Erick and I enjoyed an Italian-themed repast and left a generous tip for the young single mom who, entirely at our prompting, recounted most of her life story as she served us dinner.

We returned to the Hampton Inn only an hour and a half after we left. But that turned out to be too long. And it also turned out that all of those ridiculous rituals I performed with Simba before I took off for dinner in Las Vegas weren't that ridiculous after all. Because when I didn't watch over Simba as he ate his dinner… and I didn't lie down next to him and babble baby talk at him… and I didn't stroke his giant furry head until he fell asleep and started snoring… and I didn't sneak out of the room so he didn't realize I was gone, Simba panicked and let loose at both ends. And he repaid the Hampton Inn's hospitality with a small pile of dog vomit and a somewhat larger pool of urine that had soaked into the carpet. What's more, Simba didn't really look that good. He wasn't smiling like he usually did, and his panting was more pronounced.

When I saw—or more accurately, smelled—what happened, I sat on the floor and held Simba in my arms for a while, stroking his neck until he fell asleep. Then I set to work with two wet washcloths, two bath towels, a little bar of soap, and a tiny bottle of shampoo trying to clean up the mess he made.

The next morning Simba failed to rouse me at five like he had the previous two mornings. So when I got up on my own at seven, I had to gently shake him awake. And again, he looked subdued. At first I thought I might be overreacting. After all, he had only peed on the rug and thrown up a little from separation anxiety—so maybe it wasn't the end of the world. And he might be melancholy now because he was still embarrassed over the previous evening's faux pas. But then when I poured his breakfast, Simba just looked at it and shuffled away like he did when he first contracted his snout infection. And that, I figured, was a very bad sign.

My first instinct was to call Laureen in New York so I could share my anxiety and solicit her advice. But then I remembered how much pressure she was enduring in her new job. So I decided not to make things worse. I mean, I called Laureen anyway, but when I spoke to her, I told her that everything was fine. And that Erick and I were having a great time on the road and that we were actually slightly ahead of schedule. And when she asked how Simba was doing, I only vaguely alluded to his condition, saying, "Well, he does seem a little tired."

"That makes sense," Laureen replied. "It's probably hard for him being stuck in the back of the station wagon all day."

"Yeah, that's probably it," I said. Then I deftly steered the conversation away from Simba by asking her about her new job—a tactic that always works. Fifteen minutes later, I closed the conversation by saying, "So in terms of distance, we're now more than halfway to New York. So if all goes well, we should be rolling into town right on schedule—maybe even a day early if we don't spend two nights in Pittsburgh."

"Can't wait," said Laureen. "I love you."

I told Laureen that I loved her, too, and that I missed her, which I did. And after I hung up, I didn't feel particularly guilty about withholding bad news from her because it was basically for her own good. And besides, I could always fill her in later—when Simba felt better and she wouldn't have to fret. I was much more straightforward with Erick, who was integral to the mission. After we climbed back into the station wagon, I told him about Simba's accident and how he wouldn't eat breakfast, and I asked him what he thought we should do.

"Whatever you think is best," said Erick. "But to me this seems like a wait-and-see situation. Maybe Simba really is sick. Or maybe he just got lonely while we were out for dinner. That's happened before, right?"

I nodded and said, "Yeah, sometimes it happens when we go up to Tahoe."

"So why don't we just drive to Little Rock today as originally planned. And if Simba seems okay when we get there, we can check out the Clinton Library. Then we can spend the night in Memphis, and take a two-hour Graceland tour tomorrow morning. After that, we'll head straight to Pittsburgh."

"The only problem with that," I replied, "is that I don't think we should leave Simba alone anymore. Not even for a few hours. And I'm pretty sure they're not going to let him inside the Clinton Library. And he definitely won't be able to traipse around Graceland."

Then Erick got that telltale twinkle in his eye again, and I thought, "Really? What could he possibly have up his sleeve that would address *this* problem?"

"So I was poking around the internet last night," Erick said. "And I found a place called the Raines Road Animal Hospital in

Memphis. They take care of dogs while their owners visit Graceland. And you don't have to feel guilty about leaving Simba there because, hey, it's a vet's office. And that's probably the best place for him right now."

"Thanks, Erick. That's a great solution," I said. "I should probably call them now and make an appointment. And they can check Simba out and see if there's anything seriously wrong with him—I mean, aside from all the stuff we already know about.

"By the way," I asked, "how much does it cost?" I figured Graceland was a popular tourist destination, so I'd be paying top dollar.

"That's the best part," said Erick. "It's only ten bucks."

"So maybe three hours at ten bucks an hour plus the check-up will come to what? A $100 . . . $125. That's not too bad."

"No," said Erick. "It's ten bucks for the entire day."

That seemed beyond fair. So while Erick drove toward Little Rock, Arkansas, I booked an appointment for Simba at Raines Road Animal Hospital, which was less than a mile up Elvis Presley Boulevard from Graceland.

When we got to Little Rock, it was hot—Bakersfield hot—maybe ninety-five degrees, maybe a hundred, but with a lot more humidity. Basically, it was a sauna. So when we pulled into the big parking lot outside the Clinton Presidential Center at one thirty in the afternoon, Erick and I knew we had to somehow bust Simba into its big air-conditioned lobby.

The massive cantilevered glass-and-steel structure that housed the Clinton Library looked sort of like an alien spaceship that had inadvertently landed in a small southern town. (I know it's supposed to look like a bridge, but I'm going to go with spaceship here.) And as we walked toward the spaceship's front hatch, I mentally rehearsed my arguments for letting Simba inside. "He's old. He's sick. Don't worry. He'll just lie quietly on the floor. Believe me: he won't cause any trouble. Hey, he's a Democrat." Y'know, that sort of thing.

And to my great surprise, when we attempted to board the spaceship with Simba in tow, my charming line of crap actually seemed to work. The kindhearted older lady who was guarding the front door was just about to let Simba and me sit on a bench in a remote corner of the lobby when a stocky fellow in a blue blazer—or maybe it was gray, I don't remember—strode over, wagging his finger, and he laid down the law, the big jerk. And the law, simply put, was: No dogs allowed. So first I sat on a bench in a shady spot outside the front door with Simba and his water bowl while Erick toured the spaceship. Then Erick stayed with Simba while I went inside.

The Clinton Presidential Center was much larger and far slicker than I expected. I guess the Clintons have never really had much trouble raising money. But in terms of content, there were no major surprises. In 2012, I put together a book called *The Clintons: Their Story in Photographs* for Barnes & Noble's in-house publisher, Sterling. And the Clinton Presidential Center was kind enough to provide a few dozen images that appear in the book. So I was grateful for that. And while I was producing the book, I spent three or four months researching the Clintons' life and times. So I had a reasonably good frame of reference for the many interesting exhibits I saw inside the spaceship. And honestly, it was fun peering into the world's only full-size replica of the Oval Office and then walking around a reproduction of Clinton's cabinet room.

But I didn't want to leave Erick and Simba steaming outside in the Arkansas sauna too long. So I practically ran from exhibit to exhibit. I only glanced, for example, at the six or seven saxophones world leaders bestowed upon our forty-second president. And I spent a mere five or six minutes scanning the very long, lavishly illustrated timeline of the Clinton presidency that ran the length of the spaceship and was cast, as you might imagine, in the best possible light.

After about twenty minutes, I disembarked from the spaceship with the same general feeling about the Clintons with which I entered it. That is, that the Clintons are a remarkable larger-than-life combination of mostly good intentions and truly remarkable achievements—all richly chronicled in the presidential center—along with a whole mess of vaguely shady stuff—not nearly as well chronicled in the presidential center—constantly bubbling beneath the surface.

And every so often the shady stuff—Gennifer Flowers (1992), Travelgate (1993), Vince Foster (1993), Whitewater (1994), the missing Rose Law Firm billing records (1996), Paula Jones (1997), Monica Lewinsky (1997–1998), the Marc Rich pardon (1999), and in more recent years, fishy contributions to the Clinton Foundation and Hillary's secret email account—every so often some of that shady stuff percolates out of the muck and trips the Clintons up for a while. But then—Alakazam!—every single time (at least thus far) the Clintons manage to stand up, brush themselves off, and move forward with aplomb. Then they achieve even more remarkable things.

And believe me, if you put all of the shady stuff off to one side, Bill Clinton's eight years in the White House constitute a glorious cavalcade of remarkable achievement—economic expansion, reduced unemployment, sharply reduced crime rates, welfare reform, curtailed government spending, and the biggest budget surplus in American history—to name just a few of the biggies. And to those of you who say that President Clinton doesn't deserve credit for all of that—that it was just an historical anomaly—let me remind you that if all of those things had gone south instead, you would have been the first to cast blame.

Actually, the story of the Clintons is sort of like a Greek tragedy that almost, but never quite, reaches its *catastrophe*—and I use that word in its formal sense to mean the inevitable bad ending of all Greek tragedies. I'm probably not the first person to draw this analogy, but consider the following: our protagonists, Bill and Hillary Clinton, are bold and basically decent folks with conspicuous flaws. (Big flaws are a necessary prerequisite for tragic heroes.) And, of course, they have more than their fair share of the requisite *hubris*. They make giant hubristic blunders—called *hamartia* in Greek tragedy. Then, shrilly rebuked by a chorus of braying conservatives, they are forced to confront the error of their ways as their world crumbles around them.

But that's just it. Time and again, over the course of decades, the Clintons are felled by the assorted *hamartias* that arise from their tragic flaws—lust, arrogance, carelessness, whatever. But their world simply refuses to crumble around them—like it's supposed to in a Greek tragedy. Sometimes it comes close—like Bill's impeachment trial or the Gennifer Flowers affair that nearly derailed his first presidential campaign. But in the end, there's never a full-blown *catastrophe*—just a series of incipient and not-so-incipient public embarrassments followed in quick succession by canny maneuvers, narrow escapes, and legalistically parsed words. ("It depends upon what the meaning of the word *is* is.") So the audience—we, the American people—never experience the cleansing *catharsis* that is, after all, the whole damn point of Greek tragedy. And the Clintons, bespattered but unbowed, stride forward once more, making their mark on America and the world—not always, but quite often, for the better.

I'm pretty sure this is not the intended effect of the Clinton Presidential Spaceship. And please don't get me wrong. I respect the Clintons, admire their moxie, and appreciate their generally good intentions. But the whole Greek tragedy thing—that's kind of how I felt before I boarded the spaceship. And that's how I felt when I disembarked. And, besides, they really should have let Simba in out of the hot Arkansas sun because, damn it, that would have been the decent thing to do. I'm talking to you, you big heartless jerk in the blue or possibly gray blazer.

I have a confession to make. I'm a smug New York-slash-San Francisco jackass. And as such, I fully intended to visit Graceland "ironically," as the equally smug Brooklyn-slash-Mission hipsters say. Before I ever set foot in Graceland, I thought I knew all about it. I knew, for example, that Graceland had a ridiculous "Jungle Room," with an appalling green shag rug and a bunch of ersatz tiki nonsense. I knew there was a big gaudy car collection at Graceland, including the famous pink Cadillac that Elvis bought for his mother despite the fact she couldn't drive. And I knew that many of Elvis's weirdly bedazzled jumpsuits from his glitzy Vegas years[13] were on display in Graceland's former racquetball court—along with like a zillion gold and platinum records. So, bottom line, I expected to tour Elvis Presley's tacky mansion and its garish grounds all the while sniggering at the tasteless Tupelo hillbilly who may have been the King of Rock 'n' Roll but, let's face it, had a lot more money than taste.

And, boy, did I get my comeuppance. Because Graceland was… well, Graceland was deeply moving, actually.

Once we designated Hampton Inns as the official hotel provider for the 2014 Simba Cross-Country Death Race, I noticed they were pretty much everywhere. In fact, there were no fewer than twelve Hampton Inns in the greater Memphis area alone. So we picked one that was relatively close to Graceland and spent the night there.

---

[13] Yes, some of Elvis's suits, most notably a $10,000 gold lamé number, were tailored by old Nudie Cohn.

Simba ate most of his dinner and seemed to be rallying across the board. So that was a relief. And the next morning, we drove him to Raines Road Animal Hospital, a small veterinary clinic with a sweet middle-aged Southern lady behind the check-in counter.

After she greeted us warmly, I told her that Simba was nearly fourteen years old and had a paralyzed larynx, that he had been sick to his stomach the night before last, and that his illness was due either to separation anxiety or something much worse, perhaps a recurrence of his snout infection. Finally, I told her that even though Simba seemed to be feeling better now, I was still concerned. So could they please give him a good looking over while Erick and I toured Graceland?

"Don't worry," she said. "We'll take real good care of Simba."

And I have to say that everything about the place suggested they would. A nice young nurse emerged from the back room, knelt beside Simba, and graciously introduced herself. Then she snapped a leash onto his collar and led him away. And Simba, who never really minded going to the vet, was delighted to accompany her.

Erick and I jumped back in the car, drove down Elvis Presley Boulevard, and turned left into the massive parking lot behind the visitor center. We decided not to shell out $77 apiece for the Graceland Elvis Entourage VIP Tour, which would have let us jump the line at the mansion. But we did buy the $45 "Platinum + Airplanes Tour" so we could visit not only the mansion itself, but also Elvis's car collection and both of his jets—the airliner-sized *Lisa Marie* and the *Hound Dog II*, a smaller executive jet that was apparently the King's backup ride.

Oddly, we had to take a small bus from one side of Elvis Presley Boulevard, where the visitor center was, to the other side, where the mansion was. And when we pulled up in front of Graceland—the second-most-visited home in America after the White House—I was surprised to find a relatively staid and tasteful Classical Revival house. Graceland was large but not massive. It was the sort of mansion you might find in an old-money southern suburb. At first I was a bit disappointed because I was expecting a lot more flash. But then I remembered that Elvis didn't actually build this house. He bought it from a local doctor when he first hit the jackpot. "Just wait until we get inside," I thought, "Then we'll see some real hillbilly chic."

But when we did get inside, the entrance hall with its grand staircase and chandelier, its white-on-white living room with stained glass peacock windows, and its formal dining room with gold-trimmed royal blue curtains and elaborate silver and china collections were all quite lovely actually. Sure, there were a few unconventional touches—like, yes, the green shag carpet in the Jungle Room and the multicolored fabric concoction that shrouded the walls and ceiling of the billiards room. And, yes, it was all a bit heavy on the gilt for my particular taste. But first of all, Elvis moved into this posh crib with his parents in 1957 when he was only twenty-two years old. And secondly, he lived there during the course of two decades—the sixties and seventies—that weren't characterized by restrained elegance, particularly where rock stars were concerned. And finally, if you took all the rooms in Graceland and considered them together with the surprisingly comprehensive memorabilia collection laid out in the adjacent "Trophy Building," they told a beautiful only-in-America story about a young man who turned out to be—in composer-conductor Leonard Bernstein's words—"the greatest cultural force in the twentieth century" and, all things considered (and there is much to consider), a remarkably sympathetic character.

Graceland told the story of a poor kid born in a two-room shotgun shack in rural northeast Mississippi. A kid whose twin brother was stillborn and whose dad, Vernon, couldn't hold a job, so the family was always on what used to be called "relief." It told the story of a kid who moved to a public housing project in Memphis when he was thirteen and who wanted to sing so badly that he hung out all day on Beale Street window shopping at Lansky's where all the country music stars bought their elaborately spangled costumes. (Okay, now I get the jumpsuits.)

But the kid couldn't afford fancy costumes. In fact, he couldn't even afford a guitar. And even if he could, he was painfully shy. And pretty much everyone who was supposed to know about such things told him he was a lousy singer. Heck, he even failed his high school music class.

But after years of hard work—driving a truck while he sang on the side—the kid became globally famous. And when he did, he sold millions of records and made zillions of dollars, and teenage girls fainted just at the sight of him. And some called him the King. But others called him the devil. And gangs of teenage boys would try to beat him up after his concerts. And when he finally appeared on the all-important *Ed Sullivan Show*—only after its stone-faced host was forced to book him by popular demand—he was burned in effigy in Nashville and St. Louis. And the Catholic bishop of La Crosse, Wisconsin, sent FBI director J. Edgar Hoover an ominous letter warning him that Elvis Presley was "a definite danger to the security of the United States."

Then in 1958, at the height of his renown, the kid, now twenty-three, was drafted into the army. And even though he was convinced that two years out of the spotlight would end his career, he didn't try to weasel out of it. And he spurned repeated offers to join "Special Services," where he could have done his time performing for the troops. Nope, even though the kid was pretty much the biggest star on the planet, he wanted to serve his country as a run-of-the-mill G.I. (sort of).

And, yes, I know all of that was part of a larger public relations strategy hatched by his wily handler, "Colonel" Tom Parker (né Andreas Cornelis van Kuijk of the Netherlands). And, yes, Elvis didn't actually live in Ray Barracks in Friedberg, Germany, with the rest of his company, which doesn't really help my case here. But he did donate his Army pay to charity. And he used some of his own cash to buy television sets and extra fatigues for the guys in his outfit. And he actually showed up for work every morning at six sharp and drove a jeep all day.

And when the kid was honorably discharged two years later, he seamlessly resumed his career as a rock 'n' roll idol and movie star, billed above the title on more than thirty films. And all the while, he took care of his family and his posse. And all the while, he was remarkably philanthropic, performing free concerts, supporting more than fifty Memphis area charities, and giving away a bunch of cars, including his Rolls Royce Phantom V, to help kids' causes. He even bought FDR's presidential yacht, the *Potomac*, so he could turn around and donate it to Danny Thomas's St. Jude Children's Research Hospital.

Hey, I know Elvis Presley was no saint—not even close. And his manager, Colonel Parker, was just short of a carnival barker, which he literally was at one point. And, yes, Elvis started dating his future wife, Priscilla, in Germany when she was fourteen years old, which is admittedly pretty pervy, even for a guy from northern Mississippi. And, yes, he screwed around prolifically like every other rock star on the planet. And, yes, near the end of his relatively short life, Elvis Presley devolved into a bloated, lyric-slurring, drug-addled caricature of himself.

And when he died face down on the cold tile floor of his Graceland bathroom at age forty-two, Elvis Presley, who once asked for—and received—an authentic federal Bureau of Narcotics badge from President Nixon, had fourteen powerful pharmaceuticals in his system including Seconal, Placidyl, Valmid, Tuinal, and Demerol—a witch's brew of sedatives, barbiturates, and painkillers. But, hey, you try making the treacherous passage from backcountry yokel to global superstar while you're still in your twenties, and let's see how you do.

Anyway, I had these mostly warmhearted thoughts about Elvis Presley—whose music I never particularly loved—after touring what is, at the end of the day, his beautiful family home, a shrine to the King and, yes, a very slick money machine. But when you finish touring the mansion and the vast display of relics in the Trophy

Building, you end up in what's called the Meditation Garden. And buried there next to a lovely fountain surrounded by well-tended plantings are Elvis's dad, Vernon, his beloved mother, Gladys, and, of course, the King himself. And over to the right of the King, just on the other side of Vernon, is a fourth plaque commemorating Elvis's stillborn twin, Jesse, whose body lies in an unmarked grave back in Tupelo, because Vern and Gladys didn't have enough money for a gravesite or a headstone.

And all around the King's grave and continuing down both sides of the path that leads back to the bus stop are literally scores of floral arrangements—some quite elaborate, others mounted on easels with glittery hand-drawn placards, and all sent by ardent fans and loyal fan clubs around the globe. And every one of these folksy heartfelt oblations attest to the boundless joy Elvis gave unto the world—a hunka, hunka burning love that still blazes brightly four decades after his very unpleasant demise. And you know what? When I walked out of Graceland and got back on the bus, I was still a smug New York-slash-San Francisco jackass—but not about Elvis Presley.

Now it was time to make a run for it. After Buck Owens' crystal-less Crystal Palace, the gustatory indignities of Sonic Drive-In, and the exquisitely austere Mojave Desert; after the tallest thermometer in the world (probably) and the tallest cross in the Western Hemisphere (probably not); after scammy Zzyzx and bird-scorching Ivanpah; after Simba's Las Vegas walk of fame and the Venetian Hotel Panic Incident; after the less-than-apocalyptic high-country rainstorm, magnificent Meteor Crater, and standin' on a corner in Winslow, Arizona; after the enchanted Petrified Forest, the El Rancho's faded glory, and sad, boozy little Gallup, New Mexico; after the sublimely absurd Cadillac Ranch and tiny Erick, Oklahoma; after Simba's anxiety-induced illness and paying homage to Slick Willie and the King at their respective Ozymandian shrines—after all of that, a switch clicked in my brain, and I no longer wanted to press my luck when it came to Simba's continued survival—or my mother's. I no longer wanted to stop anywhere else or see anything else or do anything else except get myself to Pittsburgh to see my mother and get Simba to New York to see Laureen and the girls.

I don't know precisely what flipped that switch. The ghastly phone conversation with my dad in Gallup was certainly a factor. As was Simba's upset stomach in Oklahoma City. But most likely it was the Presley family cemetery at the tail end of the Graceland tour. There's nothing like a visit to the graveyard—however small—to remind us of the inevitable mortality that relentlessly stalks both dogs and men. So, like I said, now it was time to make a run for it.

The moment we finished our poignant Graceland tour, Erick and I hopped back in the station wagon and drove back over to Raines Road Animal Hospital. Erick stayed in the car while I went inside to retrieve Simba. The receptionist buzzed the back room. And while I waited for Simba to emerge, I asked the receptionist how he was doing. She told me in her melodic Tennessee accent that Simba was "doin' just fine"—which, of course, came as a relief. But she didn't provide much in the way of detail. And frankly, I should have questioned her more closely. I should have asked her, for example, whether the vet had noticed any lingering effects from Simba's kennel cough. And whether his paralyzed larynx seemed to be getting any worse. But honestly, the receptionist told me exactly what I wanted to hear—Simba was "doin' just fine"—so I didn't dig more deeply.

I did ask for the tab, which came to precisely ten dollars. And I did ask the receptionist why there was no additional charge for examining Simba. To which she replied, "Well, he seemed to be okay, so we didn't really have to do anything." And I guess that, too, should have been a red flag. But again it was exactly what I wanted to hear. So I pulled a ten-dollar bill from my wallet and thanked the nice lady for her kind hospitality. Then we gently loaded Simba into the station wagon and drove back onto I-40 headed east once more toward Nashville. In Nashville, we merged onto I-65 and drove 170 miles north to Louisville, Kentucky. Then we switched over to I-71, which took us the rest of the way across the Bluegrass State.

I don't recall very much about our quick sprint across Kentucky—although I can tell you from previous visits that it's a very beautiful place, at least the parts I've seen. All I remember about our drive that day is that there were lots of billboards along the side of the highway. And some of those billboards invited Erick and me to visit sex shops conveniently located near several exits, while others urged us to accept Jesus Christ as our personal savior. I honestly don't know whether the local porn peddlers and the neighborhood bible thumpers were consciously duking it out for the hearts and souls of Interstate motorists. But the alternating porn and Jesus billboards made for a very yin-yang sort of drive, morally speaking.

And to make that drive even more surreal, Erick and I heard several radio commercials that first spoke in menacing tones about ISIS militants who were beheading people in Iraq and then suggested—apparently as a logical consequence—that we should arm ourselves with the reasonably priced used firearms available at their well-stocked weapons emporium. The connection between ISIS savagery in the far-off Levant and buying a used gun in Kentucky was, of course, tenuous. But the gun store commercials seemed to offer up the same sort of easy-to-grasp, good-versus-evil dichotomy as the billboards. Buy a gun and protect yourself from ISIS. Come to Jesus and protect yourself from porn. Build a big wall and protect yourself from job-stealing Mexican rapists. Oh, wait, that last one's Donald Trump.

At any rate, we were now in a hurry. So we had neither the time nor the inclination to visit any porn shops, however conveniently located. And despite the fair warning, it seemed unlikely that we would encounter any ISIS militants in central Kentucky. So Erick and I let all of the contradictory messaging wash right over us. And after eight hours on the road, we ran out of steam in Cincinnati, Ohio, which was blessed with no fewer than eight Hampton Inns.

Simba had another good night—his second in a row—probably because I ate dinner in the room with him and slept by his side. And the next morning, he was back to his old up-and-at-'em-at-the-crack-of-dawn self. In order to get to Pittsburgh that day, we had to drive the 230-mile breadth of Ohio and then cross a 15-mile sliver of West Virginia. But that would only take four hours. And thanks to Simba we got an early start.

By noon, we found ourselves emerging into eye-blinking daylight from Pittsburgh's half-mile long Fort Pitt Tunnel. The tunnel deposited us directly onto the Fort Pitt Bridge. And from there, we had a magnificent view of the Steel City's dozen or so skyscrapers, which occupy a compact triangle of land bounded by two wide rivers—the Monongahela and Allegheny—that merge at that point to form the mighty Ohio. For my money, it's the most beautiful cityscape in America—but I'm a born-and-bred western PA guy, so take that with a grain of salt. At any rate, less than twenty minutes later, I was knocking on my parents' apartment door. And what I found on the other side of that door was deeply disturbing.

In my own defense, I had called my mother every day religiously for the past two years. And I did fly my dad out to San Francisco in April so we could spend ten days together. And of course, I had been super busy jetting back and forth between San Francisco and New York, trying to facilitate our cross-country move. Actually, if I really put my mind to it, I could probably come up with any number of valid excuses for not visiting my ailing eighty-four-year-old mother for the last six months. But the fact of the matter was, I hadn't visited her for six months. And the moment I walked through the door, I knew I should have come sooner.

I was greeted by one of the small cadre of home health-care workers who now took turns trying to keep my very demanding mother as comfortable as possible from noon to eight p.m. each day. And since the agency sent a different young woman every three or four days—likely to keep them from quitting—I had never met the particular young blonde woman in blue hospital scrubs who let me in. So I introduced myself. Then I glanced around the apartment, and my heart sank.

My parents' home, which had always been a warm and welcoming place, was no longer bright and cheerful—even with its rose-colored carpet, sunny yellow sofa, and bold, colorful prints crowding the walls. Now it looked dingy and disorganized—sort of dirty actually—with two walkers, two wheelchairs, and an oxygen tank caddy all jumbled together along one wall of the living room. There were dark, grimy spots on the rose-colored carpet and several long white scrapes across the pink wallpaper in the hallway where the wheelchair had apparently rubbed up against it.

I asked Erick if he wouldn't mind waiting in the living room with Simba for a moment while I went back to my parents' bedroom to let them know I was there. I walked down the long hallway with a distinct sense of dread. And halfway to the bedroom, I heard my father yell from inside the hall bathroom that he would be out in a minute.

"Okay, Dad," I yelled back. "Take your time."

"I won't be long, Dov," he said. (He was the only person who called me that.) "I'm just finishing up in here, so I'll see you in a few minutes."

But I knew that probably wouldn't be true because, over the course of the past two years, my father's Parkinson's disease had progressed to the point where something as simple as brushing his teeth and shaving could take more than thirty minutes, and getting dressed in the morning consumed the better part of an hour.

When I walked into the bedroom—where my mother now spent twenty-two hours in bed every day—it was dark and stuffy, despite the yellow wallpaper and red and yellow drapes. For some reason the drapes were drawn in the middle of the day, so the only light in the room emanated from the forty-watt lamp on my mother's bedside table. As my eyes adjusted to the gloom, I saw my mother lying on her back above the covers in a beige nightgown with her eyes closed and an oxygen tube up her nose. The clear plastic tube led down the side of the bed and across the floor to a mini-fridge-size concentrator that was buzzing and huffing away inside a small walk-in closet. I also noticed that there was now an aluminum railing on my mother's side of the bed to keep her from rolling off onto the floor, which had apparently happened a dozen times. And as usual, the television was blaring C-SPAN, since my mother was one of the fifty or so people in America who were implausibly riveted by hour-long House votes on agricultural appropriation bills.

As I approached my mother's bed, she opened her eyes, looked up, and smiled wanly. "Oh, David. You're here," she said in a soft, happy tone.

But she didn't sit up, probably because she couldn't.

"How was your trip?" she asked.

"So far, it's been great," I replied, as cheerfully as possible under the circumstances. "Simba seems to be doing pretty well—at least for now. And Erick and I visited lots of really interesting places. We went to Graceland yesterday. And I'm going to tell you all about it, but first things first. How are *you* doing?"

My mother looked at me without speaking for a moment. Then her eyes filled with tears, and she started sobbing. She cried a lot these days, nearly every time I spoke to her on the phone. But now that we were face-to-face, I could see that these were tears of pure helplessness… and hopelessness. And without any words, only tears, I knew that the answer to my stupid question, "How are you doing?" was "I'm doing about as badly as possible. And I feel as if I've fallen into a deep pit and that I'll never crawl out of it. And I'm in constant pain from my spinal stenosis, despite the four operations. And I sneak extra OxyContin pills whenever I can badger one of the girls into smuggling them past your father. And if I can get my hands on it, which is difficult, I wash the OxyContin down with vodka, so for a few hours, at least, I can keep the pain and the misery at bay.

"And worst of all, my failing heart can no longer clear enough fluid from my lungs for the oxygen to get in. So I am literally drowning in slow motion. And I'm tethered by a forty-foot hose to that buzzing, wheezing machine in the closet. And once a week or so, the hose gets kinked or I roll over and pull the tube out of the machine. And I don't notice it at first. But after a few minutes I do notice that I can't breathe. So I yell for someone to come and help me. And so far, someone has always come. But now I live in constant fear that, one day, no one will get here in time. And if that happens, I'll slip into death. Because that buzzing, wheezing machine is now all that stands between me and suffocation."

And what can you say to that, except "I love you, Mom," and "I'm sorry you have to live in constant pain. And I'm sorry that you now take powerful narcotics that dim your bright and nimble mind. And I'm sorry that you of all people—our own goddamn force of nature—now have to lie here helplessly in the shadows.

"We always joked, Mom, that you sucked all the oxygen out of the room. But soon all the oxygen in the world won't be enough to keep you alive.

"And you know what, Mom? If the truth be told, I'm also pretty mad at you. I'm angry that you never did your back exercises after your spinal stenosis operations. And that you never did the breathing exercises after your mitral valve replacement. And that you refused to go to rehab like everyone else in the whole goddamn world who has ever had a mitral valve replacement. The doctors told you this would happen if you didn't go to rehab. We begged you to go. So why didn't you do it, Mom? Why did you let this happen to you?

"But in the end, Mom, I am indescribably sorry that this is the way you're going to die—slowly drowning over the course of months. You had a good life, Mom—a husband who proposed to you on your first date and relentlessly adored you every day of your life for the past six decades—even when you weren't easy to adore; two happy, healthy sons; eight beautiful grandchildren; and a coterie of loyal friends.

"You had a good life, Mom. But you will not have a good death. Your death will come down to the incremental turning of a little black plastic knob on the oxygen concentrator—from eight to nine when eight isn't enough, then from nine to ten when nine isn't enough. And then one day, ten won't be enough. And you will die."

But of course I didn't say any of those things. All I said was, "Hey, come on now. What's all this crying? You need to pull yourself together, Mom. Erick and Simba are waiting in the living room. And they want to come in and say hello."

"Oh, that's wonderful," my mother said, wiping the tears from her cheek. "I've always liked Erick."

"Okay, then," I said in a mock stern tone. "You pull yourself together. And I'll go get them."

I walked out of my mother's bedroom and stopped halfway down the hall for a moment so I could shed a few tears myself. Then

I dragged the back of my wrist across my eyes so Erick wouldn't see I'd been crying.

When Erick, Simba, and I went back into the bedroom—after I warned Erick that it wasn't pretty in there—Simba lay at the foot of the bed. And Erick and I stood next to my mother telling her tales from the road. And my mother hung on every word as if we were recounting our journey to Mars or a voyage to Atlantis. And that reminded me—at a moment when I really needed to be reminded—that no one ever will care as much about the minutia of my life as my mother. Nor will anyone ever be as steadfastly loyal, although Laureen comes close.

Fifteen minutes later, my father finally walked into the bedroom and greeted Erick and me in his usual courtly fashion. Actually "walked into the room" isn't really the right description. "Shuffled into the room" would be more accurate. Because since I'd last seen him, my father's Parkinson's had noticeably progressed. And when I saw him drag his feet across the carpet and when I saw his legs freeze up against his will ("C'mon you so-and-so's," he'd say to his legs) I knew that caring for my mother and constantly worrying about her was taking a terrible toll.

I also knew from the way she spoke to him that my mother had decided to simply ignore the whole Parkinson's situation so she could continue to demand my father's unwavering attention. And that, too, was a problem. Because even with a health-care aide in the apartment from noon to eight, that still left sixteen hours a day, every day, when my dad was her sole retainer—the only person who dispensed her pills, fetched her endless glasses of Diet Sprite she didn't drink, brought her snacks she didn't eat, and did the dozens of other random tasks that flitted across my her mind at the rate of three or four per hour.

When my mother wanted to satisfy one of these whims, she had two methods of summoning my father. The most common was simply bellowing, "Norm! Norm!" over and over at the top of her lungs. But if that didn't work, she repeatedly buzzed an intercom system that had recently been installed in every room of the apartment.

During the mere day and a half I was in Pittsburgh, I tried to help my dad as much as I could. And whenever my mother bellowed his name, I would immediately yell, "Don't worry, Dad, I got this." But even then, there were a few tasks that only he could do. And whenever my dad shuffled into the bedroom to find out what it was my mother wanted and then shuffled off again, my mother would turn to me and say, in an exasperated tone, "You have no idea how slow your father is these days. I thought he was slow before, but now it's unbelievable." And she said this as if my father didn't have Parkinson's disease, or if he did, it was certainly no excuse.

And if all that weren't enough to convince me that my parents' daily lives had devolved into a dark mire of pain and dysfunction, their sweet neighbor from down the hall, ninety-year-old Lois O'Conner, made it a point to pull me aside in the hallway and tell me, "David, your father shouldn't be taking care of Hannah anymore. You know he's got the Parkinson's. So someone should be taking care of *him*. And unless you and your brother do something very soon, this is going to kill him."

Then she stared me straight in the eye to let me know that she was serious and that if I failed to act, my father's death would be on me. And, again, I didn't say what I was thinking, which was, "You're talking to me as if I didn't already know that, Mrs. O'Conner. As if I hadn't discussed this endlessly with my brother. As if we hadn't repeatedly told my father, 'You know, Dad, you've really got to get some more help around here. You've got the money, so what's the problem? You're like a frog in water that's been heated so slowly you don't realize it's boiling.'"

And as if my dad hadn't replied every single time, "Well, I'd like to, Dov, but you know your mother doesn't like strangers in the apartment all day."

But, again, I didn't say any of that to sweet old Lois O'Conner, who was, of course, basically right. All I said was, "I understand what you're saying. And, believe me, I'm doing everything I can."

But that too was a lie. Because it was actually my younger brother, Dan, who lived four blocks away with his wife and three children, who was doing, if not everything he could, then certainly more than I did. I did the easy stuff like calling every day and buying my dad thoughtful Parkinson's-related gifts like easy-button shirts and a big motorized recliner that lifted him out of the seat and massaged his back. But whenever my mother or father had to go to the doctor's office—which was at least twice a week—it was my brother who took them. And whenever my mother rolled onto the floor or fell down in the bathroom in the middle of the night, it was my brother who got the call. And when the hotel that was closest to my parents' apartment—alas, not a Hampton Inn—wouldn't admit Simba, it was Dan and his wife, Stacy, who let him stay overnight with their three kids and Brody, their six-year-old cockapoo.

The second evening I was in Pittsburgh, my father decided that all of us—my mother, my brother, his wife, their three children, Erick, and I—should go out to dinner at a fancy steakhouse in downtown Pittsburgh. That meant, of course, that Simba would have to stay at my brother's house, alone with Brody the cockapoo, which wasn't optimal. But I figured having another dog around might tamp down Simba's separation anxiety. And attending what might be my last dinner out with my mother would have to trump Simba's needs, at least for one evening.

It also meant that we had to mount a fairly complex logistical operation to get my parents to the restaurant. In terms of equipment, the mission required a wheelchair for my mother and a walker for my dad, three large oxygen tanks that would hopefully keep my mother alive and breathing for the three hours we would be away from the apartment, a pull cart for the oxygen tanks, two small pillows to make the wheelchair more comfortable, a regulator, and the little wrench that we would use to change out the tanks. The pre-dinner operation alone took several hours, including half an hour to load my parents and all of their equipment into two cars.

In many ways, Pittsburgh is a small town, particularly the Jewish community. And as my mother passed in her wheelchair from the front door to the back of the restaurant, where our table was, she discovered, to her great delight, that she knew several other couples dining there. Most of my mother's close friends had died during the past three or four years. So the people she recognized were more like acquaintances. And they were all a bit younger than she was—maybe in their mid-seventies.

My mother had always been a raging extrovert—an only child who got all the attention at home, then a beautiful young woman who captivated all the high school and college boys. And she had always been the life of the party—sometimes to a fault. Like the time forty years ago when she poured a drink over the head of a guy she didn't like at a cocktail party and then cried out for all to hear, "The devil made me do it!"

The guy, who was a burly six foot three, rose from a now-damp sofa and challenged my father to a fistfight outside. But my father, who trained in hand-to-hand combat and knife fighting in the airborne and was a hardened veteran of more than one barroom brawl, quietly demurred. A few years later, the guy blackballed my parents at the local country club. So I guess, in the end, he won.

Anyway, as I pushed my mother's wheelchair through the restaurant, pulling one of her oxygen tanks behind me, she asked me to wheel her over to three different tables along the way. And since I was standing behind her, I could see the expressions on various diners' faces as my mother rolled up to them in her now shrunken form with an oxygen tube stuck up her nose and the big green metal oxygen tank trailing behind her. These expressions ranged from, "Holy shit! What happened to her?" to "Oh, my God. That could be me in a few years."

So even though my mother was thoroughly enjoying one of her few public appearances in the last two years, her unexpected presence at a fancy downtown eatery wasn't exactly a cause for celebration amongst the still ambulatory, breathing-all-on-their-own set who were roughly a decade behind her on the one-way road to Homewood Cemetery. And to make matters worse, my mother's conversation, which had always been smooth, effortless, even effervescent, now seemed slightly off-kilter. It was sort of like when you talk to someone with a mild mental disability, and you can't quite put your finger on it, but you definitely sense something is wrong. And that, given my mother's once agile mind and lifelong social ease, broke my heart even further.

When we finally got to our table, there were eight chairs and an empty spot at the head of the table for my mother's wheelchair. Initially, I was delighted to see that the restaurant had gotten it right, putting my mom in the place of honor. But then my mother decided that the seating arrangement wasn't exactly to her liking. She wanted to sit, instead, in the middle of the table with her back to the wall, so she could speak to everyone more easily. And perhaps more importantly, so she could see if someone else she knew walked into the restaurant.

This sudden change of plan required two waiters to carefully pull the table out from the wall without disturbing the place settings, then to remove the three chairs from that side of the table, push my mother's wheelchair into the position she wanted, and finally to put everything back together again. When that was accomplished, we all sat down and made ourselves comfortable—at which point my mother immediately announced—quite loudly actually—that she had to go to the bathroom. So the entire process had to be undone and redone again when she returned fifteen minutes later. And even though I knew it was no big deal, particularly under the circumstances, I found myself irritated that my mother seemed completely at ease ordering everyone around in a haughty fashion—particularly the poor waiters—and organizing everything precisely the way she wanted it with no regard for anyone else's preferences.

But then I put that together with her uncharacteristic social clumsiness, and I figured out what was going on. For two years, my mother had been laying in a shadowy room as her once sizable circle of friends slowly contracted—mostly because they died, but also because she couldn't attend social events anymore, and it must be said, because she now tossed off a lot of thoughtless remarks that offended even her closest friends.

So while my mother got to see my brother for an hour or so two or three times a week, and while she talked to me on the phone every day for maybe half an hour, the rest of the time she communicated only with my father and her rotating team of health-care minions. And that interaction consisted, for the most part, of her complaining about her condition, criticizing everyone's performance, and issuing mandates like a petty dictator. So, in effect, my mother had become desocialized, unable to function in polite society anymore. And her strong will—the force of nature that had always been there and had always made her interesting, even fascinating—was no longer buffered by her prodigious intellect and natural charm.

The full extent of my mother's desocialization became clearer when her first oxygen tank ran out of gas after only forty-five minutes. That was fifteen minutes sooner than anyone expected, so we weren't really ready for it. When the oxygen stopped flowing, my mother nodded off at the table. Her eyes closed, and her chin dropped to her chest. And when we woke her up and asked her if she was all right, she realized what was happening and her adrenaline kicked in. She gasped a few times and then shouted loudly, "Norm! Norm! I'm not getting any oxygen! Do something! Do something now!"

My father got a panic-stricken look on his face and hoisted himself out of his chair as quickly as he could, given the Parkinson's. His hands shook as he frantically searched through the little black bag on the oxygen caddy for the wrench to change the tank. But it wasn't there. So after a minute or so—although it seemed much longer—he said to my brother, "Hey, Dan, I don't know what happened to the little tool. Maybe it fell out in the car."

"I'll check," said my brother. And he ran through the restaurant and out the front door to his car, which was in the parking structure next door. Three or four very long minutes later, he came running back to the table with the little wrench in his hand. Then Erick the engineer took over, expertly swapping out the tanks in a matter of seconds—even though he'd never done it before.

By that point, of course, everyone in the restaurant—or at least everyone anywhere near us—was staring at our table in full-blown horror. And under normal circumstances, I would have been mortified that my mother had launched into a screaming panic attack in an upscale dining establishment.

But, honestly, what are you going to do? Are you going to get all upset because your mother is screaming for oxygen? Are you going to get embarrassed because she's been a shut-in so long she's forgotten how to talk to people? Are you going to get angry with her because she treats your father like a servant or because most of her problems are entirely of her own making?

No. You don't. You want to, at least at first. But then you remember that she has always been the most loyal mother on the face of the earth. And that at least until a few years ago, she cared more about your life than her own. You remember that you probably wouldn't have accomplished whatever you did in life without her constant nagging and her lifelong, unstinting, and entirely illogical belief that you and your brother were the smartest boys who ever lived and that the sun rose and set on you. You recognize that this is a truly gruesome chapter in her life, the part at the end. But you also realize that this ghastly interlude between life and death with all of its concomitant horrors—the yelling and screaming, the profound selfishness, the frightening appearance, the self-defeating stubbornness, the utter lack of compassion for your father—you realize all of that has to be considered in the context of her entire life. Because even though my mother would likely die very badly very soon, her life was much more than the dreadful run-up to her death. It was decades of love, support, and excitement. It was a constant sense that she was firmly in your corner, that you always had a fierce ally. And it was the constant knowledge that any room she was in would be more interesting simply because she was there.

And this was the time in her life when we, her family, would have to love her without regard to what she did or what she said or how shockingly selfish and self-centered she behaved. This was the time when we would have to love her unconditionally, like... well, you know.

Needless to say, I left Pittsburgh thoroughly depressed and deeply concerned. The whole appalling situation had been much worse than I'd expected—and I'd expected something pretty bad. But for the time being, at least, I had to prioritize my concerns. First I'd reunite Simba with Laureen and the girls. Then I'd figure out what I could do to help my parents during my mother's long slog toward death. Surprisingly, in my late fifties, no one very close to me had ever died—not since my grandparents passed away back when I was a teenager. So for me this was an unknown country.

The last leg of our cross-country journey would be relatively short—a six-hour, 374-mile sprint to the finish line. Erick and I left the Springhill Suites in Pittsburgh's East Liberty neighborhood at eight in the morning. Then we stopped by my parents' apartment to say good-bye.

Even before she was confined to her bed, my mother used to stay up most of the night reading and watching television. Eight in the morning for her was like three in the morning for most people.

And she rarely got up before eleven. So she was still asleep when Erick and I got to the apartment. And I didn't want to wake her. But my dad was up. And he met us at the door in his bathrobe and slippers. When I bent over to hug him, I remembered that he had once been six foot one and a pretty solid guy. But now, at eighty-seven, he was a full three inches shorter, stooped by age, Parkinson's, and chronic anxiety about my mother. I told my father that I loved him. And I begged him yet again to get some more help around the place. But, of course, I knew that wouldn't happen, so I guess that was more for me than for him. And I left feeling like a deserter.

I drove three blocks to my brother's house to pick up Simba. And when my brother's wife, Stacy, brought him to the front door, she said, "I don't know what he's been like the rest of the trip, but you should probably keep an eye on him. He seems really tired or maybe depressed. And he has a lot of trouble getting up and down the steps."

I chalked Simba's melancholy up to the fact that we had been separated overnight. And I knew his trouble with the stairs was arthritis, a long-standing malady. So Stacy's observations didn't particularly alarm me—especially since the alarmed part of my brain was pretty full at the moment.

I took the first shift at the wheel, driving three hours east to Harrisburg on I-76. Then Erick took over when we merged onto I-78. Two hours later, we crossed into New Jersey. When we got as far as the affluent exurb of Summit, less than an hour from Manhattan, we pulled off the interstate to get some gas and walk Simba for a while. I filled the tank while Erick went inside to use the men's room. Then I walked Simba down a small hill to a grassy area with some tall pine trees and bushes. Simba did his business in no time flat. But then, as we started hiking back up the hill toward the filling station, his legs buckled, and he collapsed in a heap on the grass.

"Uh-oh, what's going on, boy?" I said as a wave of panic washed over me.

Simba looked up at me wide-eyed, so I knew he was frightened, too. I tried to calm him by saying, "Come on, buddy, let's get you up. We're only an hour from New York, and Laureen and the girls are waiting to see you. Come on, boy. I know you can do it."

I straddled Simba and pulled up on his torso to take some of the weight off his legs as he tried to regain his footing. He got up on the third try. Then he wobbled back and forth for a moment. But he remained standing. I waited until he fully steadied himself. Then I got behind him, crouched down, and pushed his butt the rest of the way up the hill.

When we reached the gas station, Erick was just emerging from the men's room. When he saw the look on my face he said, "Hey, what's going on?"

"Simba lost his balance and fell over," I replied, "like he did when he got his snout infection last year. He's still pretty shaky, but he made it back to the car under his own steam. So maybe he's okay. But we should probably get moving."

Erick nodded and together we lifted Simba up and gently placed him on his bed in the back of the station wagon. Simba was still breathing hard, but he was also smiling—although I didn't know whether that was because he felt better or because he wanted to ingratiate himself with Erick and me so we wouldn't leave him behind like a dog pack would.

A half hour later, we were approaching Manhattan on I-95, and we had a choice. We could either take the Lincoln Tunnel under the Hudson River—in which case we would have to drive through Midtown traffic to the Upper East Side. Or we could continue twelve miles further north on I-95, cross the George Washington Bridge at the northern tip of Manhattan, and then take the FDR south to the 96th Street exit. Erick was driving, and I was navigating, so he asked me what I thought we should do. I honestly didn't know which way would be faster. And Google Maps was no help, because it showed red lines, indicating heavy traffic, on both routes. But then I recalled from my old days in Manhattan that the approach to the Lincoln Tunnel was always sort of a nightmare. Or at least that's how I remembered it. So I said to Erick, "Why don't we just take the GW? It may be less crowded."

As we drew closer to the George Washington Bridge, we saw signs that required us to make another choice—this time between the upper and the lower decks of the bridge. And again, I didn't know which way would be better. So I opted for the upper deck on the entirely irrelevant theory that it might provide a better view of the city as we triumphantly entered it. But that turned out to be a very bad call. Because once we committed to the upper deck, we saw another flashing sign indicating that there was an accident up ahead. But by that time, it was too late to change course.

I called Laureen on her cell phone. First I gave her the good news: we were only eight miles away. Then the bad news: we were mired in a massive traffic jam. I decided, at least for the time being, not to give her the really bad news—about Simba's collapse at the gas station—because I figured I could do that more sensitively in person.

"So how long do you think it'll take you to get here?" Laureen asked.

"Honestly, I have no idea," I replied. "Right now we're creeping along at one or two miles per hour. But who knows? It could clear up at any minute."

"Well the girls and I are waiting for you at the apartment," she said. "We're sitting on the floor because there's no furniture yet. But we can't wait to see you and Erick and show Simba his new home."

"And guess what?" she continued. "Since we're staying at the hotel for two more weeks while they finish painting the apartment, the staff there got everything ready for Simba's arrival. They put a dog bed in the room and left a big basket full of biscuits and treats. And since I've already been there for six weeks, the doormen all know me, and I've shown them Simba's picture. So they're really excited to meet him. They even put up a sign in the room that says, 'Welcome Simba.' Wasn't that sweet of them?"

"I guess they do that sort of thing when you stay in a hotel for two months," I said. But then I realized that sounded sort of churlish, so I added, "But, yes, that was very nice of them."

"Anyway," I continued, "I'll give you another call when we finally shake loose from this mess."

For the next full hour, we crept along at an infuriatingly sluggish pace, stopping and starting, stopping and starting. And with each passing minute, Simba's breathing seemed to become more labored. And after awhile, he was panting hard as if he couldn't get enough air. Like most people—well, maybe more than most people—I get pretty anxious when I come to a dead stop in heavy traffic and don't know when I'll start moving again. When that happens, Laureen always says she can see my blood pressure rising. But Simba's rapidly declining condition obviously made things much worse. And in my mind, I began to rail against the cruel fates that might allow Simba to travel three thousand miles across the continent to see his family only to let him die a few miles short of the goal. "That would truly suck," I thought.

I looked back over my shoulder and said to Simba, "Are you okay back there, buddy?" And like my mother, he didn't need words to tell me he wasn't. So I tried to rally his spirits with an encouraging halftime-in-the-locker-room sort of speech. And, yes, I realized he couldn't understand one word I was saying, but I thought he might be inspired by the rah-rah tone.

"Don't worry, Simba," I said. "You're not going to die in a traffic jam on the George Washington Bridge. You're going to make it to the apartment. And you're going to see Laureen and the girls. And they're all going to give you a big hug and tell you how much they love you.

"And you know why you're not going to die on this bridge, Simba? Because dying in a Sunday afternoon traffic jam on the George Washington Bridge is a bad way to go. And you're not going have a bad death like my mother. You're going to have a good death—a peaceful death in a comfortable spot with your loving family gathered all around you—because that was the whole goddamn point of this trip, Simba. And in this regard, at least, we will not fail!"

Simba seemed perplexed by my strident tone, and Erick looked slightly uncomfortable, but at least it made me feel better.

When we finally got to the other side of the bridge, we fought our way literally inch-by-inch across three lanes of traffic so we could exit onto Harlem River Drive, which turned into the FDR a few miles south. Thankfully the FDR was wide open. So we zoomed down to 96th Street. And when we got off the highway, I called Laureen again.

"Hey, we're finally in Manhattan!" I exclaimed. "Ten more minutes, honey—maybe less—and we'll be parked outside the building. So grab the girls and come on down to the street."

"We're on our way," said Laureen.

I looked back at Simba, and I said, "You hang in there, buddy. We're almost there."

But Simba didn't look very good at all. And he was panting like he just ran a mile.

Erick negotiated the relatively light traffic on 96th Street, turned left onto Park Avenue and drove seven blocks south. Then he pulled the car up in front of a fire hydrant on the southwest corner of 89th and Park. I jumped out, ran around to the back of the car, and opened the tailgate so I could hug Simba and try to calm his ragged breathing. And right at that moment, Laureen, Angela, and Grace ran out of the building and onto the sidewalk—just as I imagined eight days and three thousand miles earlier. They spotted the car and raced toward us with big smiles on their faces. They took a moment to hug Erick. Then each of them was polite enough to give me a quick hug before they got down to business and welcomed the real star of the show to his new home in Manhattan.

Laureen, Angela, and Grace squealed "Simba! Simba!" over and over again in high-pitched voices. They all hugged him in turn. And they each told him how much they missed him and cherished him. Then they showered him with love and affection as thoroughly as any dog ever has been or will be. And Simba was ecstatic, seeing his family all together again. It was a like a tonic for him. He smiled. His breathing relaxed. And after five or six minutes, he was able to hop out of the station wagon all on his own and jump around a bit with the girls on the sidewalk, his tail wagging furiously. It was clear that the love of his family was exactly the medicine Simba needed.

After the shrieks and the hugs and baby talk all ran their long course, Laureen grabbed Simba's red leash, attached it to his collar and said, "He probably has to pee. I'm going to take him over to see Central Park. It's only two blocks away, and I know he's going to love it."

I told her that Simba had done his business only a few hours earlier, so not to expect much. Then I briefly recounted his collapse at the New Jersey gas station and warned her that he had been panting pretty hard ever since. "Keep an eye on him," I said. "He's still a little wobbly."

"Don't worry," said Laureen. "I just want to show him Central Park so that he gets a good first impression of his new home. There are so many dogs over there for him to play with, especially on the weekend. I think he'll be really excited."

"Sounds good," I said. "But, hey, before you go. Where am I supposed to park?"

"There's a garage on 88th between Park and Madison," she replied. "Just leave the bags in the car. They'll be safe. And when I get back from the park, we'll take Simba up to see the apartment. Then we'll all head down to the hotel. Lisa's waiting for us there," she said, referring to Erick's wife.

"Okay, I should be able to manage that," I replied. "Have a good time with your old buddy, Simba."

"I will," said Laureen. "It's so good to finally see him… and you, of course."

Then she and Simba disappeared around the corner. And I noticed that Simba had a little bit of that old spring in his step. "Mind-body connection," I thought. "He just needed to see Laureen."

Angela and Grace headed upstairs to the empty apartment. And Erick and I got back into the car and drove around the corner to the garage. When we got there, I climbed out of the car and handed the keys to the attendant. Then I turned to Erick.

"Well, I guess we did it," I said. "It was a little hairy at the end, but thanks to you, we got Simba to New York all in one piece. We reunited him with Laureen and the girls. And now that he's seen them he seems to be feeling a lot better. Did you notice how he was jumping around with the girls? He was like a new dog."

"We should get a bottle of champagne at the hotel tonight," said Erick. "We'll drink a toast and celebrate our successful mission."

I was just about to thank Erick again from the bottom of my heart for making all of this possible when my cell phone rang. I pulled it out of my pocket and looked at the screen. It was Laureen.

"Hi, honey," I said. "What's up?"

"Something's wrong with Simba," she replied.

"What is it?"

"Can you just get over here? I'm at something called Engineer's Gate. It's at the corner of 90th and Fifth Avenue."

"Okay," I replied, "I'll get there as fast as I can." Then I hung up.

"What's going on?" asked Erick.

"I'm not sure. It sounds like Simba might be sick again. Laureen wants me to meet her at entrance to the park up on 90th Street. So I'm going to run up there now."

And without waiting for Erick, I took off as fast as I could out of the garage and onto the streets of Manhattan.

17. LUCKY DOG

Manhattan, New York
Still August 24, 2014

When I got to the entrance to Central Park—out of breath from my four-block sprint—I found a small group of New Yorkers, maybe ten or so, milling around a long semicircular concrete bench built into one of the impressive baroque piers on either side of Engineer's Gate. I didn't see Laureen. But as I got closer, I spotted Simba. He was lying on the bench on his right side with his legs sticking straight out and his big brown eyes open but unblinking. I knew right away he was gone.

But then Laureen ran up to me. And it was clear that she either didn't realize Simba was dead or, more likely, that she wasn't yet ready to accept the loss. Laureen had two young men with her, both in their mid-twenties.

"I was about a quarter mile up the bridal path," said Laureen, still pretty calm, "and Simba was having a great time playing with all the other dogs. He was like a puppy again, wagging his tail and pulling hard on the leash like he used to in the old days. He was all excited to see the horses and the people and all the action in the park and he wanted to keep going further up the path. But then he stopped to poop. And he fell over. And he couldn't get up again. He howled for fifteen or twenty seconds like he was in terrible pain. It was horrible, David. Then he passed out.

"These guys here were nice enough to carry him all the way back. But now we need to get him to a vet, David, or an animal hospital. And we need to do it right away. And I don't know where to go. Where should we go?"

The two young men who had carried Simba to the bench both looked at me. One of them shook his head discreetly to indicate that it was now too late for a vet. The eight or ten other people gathered around must also have known Simba was dead. But then Laureen walked over to the bench and knelt down to stroke her old buddy—like her child in some ways—and there was fierceness in her eyes.

"Don't worry, Simba," she said. "Everything's going to be all right. We're going to get you the hospital, and the doctors are going to help you and everything's going to be all right."

And all the people in the semicircle around the bench looked at each other and then at me. And without a word, a conspiracy of kindness formed where everyone, including me, would pretend that there was still hope for Simba.

"Well, we better get him to the pet hospital then," said one of the young men who had carried Simba to the bench.

"I'll hail a cab," said another guy in his mid-thirties wearing a plaid shirt.

"I'll help you," said yet another young man with a closely trimmed beard.

Then a middle-aged fellow in jogging clothes with his cell phone out said, "Okay, I googled it, and you should probably take him to the Animal Medical Center at 62nd and York. They're supposed to be pretty good. I'm going to call them now and tell them you're coming. What's the dog's name?"

"His name is Simba," I said.

Then the guy in the plaid shirt yelled from the street, "Hey, I got a cab here."

And without being asked, two other young men—not the ones who carried him to the bench—picked Simba up, all eighty-five pounds of him, and they lugged him over to a yellow taxi that was pulled up to the curb on the corner of Fifth Avenue and 90th Street. Then, with some difficulty, they laid him out across the backseat.

"The first cab I hailed wouldn't take him," said the guy in the plaid shirt. "He said it was against company policy. What an asshole! But this guy's okay. It's probably against his company's policy, too. But he's going to do it anyway because he's a decent human being. Give me your cell number so I can call you later," he said. Then he sidled up to me and said *sotto voce*, "Hey, look, I know the dog's dead. But it's the right thing to do."

"Thanks," I said. "Thanks for everything."

By that point, Laureen was in the backseat of the cab with Simba's head in her lap. And since they took up the entire seat I climbed up front with the driver whose name was Muhammad. I really didn't know whether Muhammad realized Simba was dead or not—and I didn't want to ask him in case Laureen was listening. But he drove very quickly through the streets of Manhattan as if we really did need to get Simba to the pet hospital as quickly as possible.

I heard Laureen call Angela on her cell phone and tell her to grab Grace, hop in a cab and get down to 62nd and York as quickly as possible.

"I'll tell you when you get there," she said.

Since it was a late August weekend, lots of New Yorkers were out of town. So traffic was light, and we got to the Animal Medical Center in less than fifteen minutes. We pulled up to the curb at a pretty good rate of speed. And to my great surprise, two guys in green scrubs literally ran out the front door of the hospital pushing a regular human-sized gurney. It was like something you'd see in a television show or movie. Maybe it was just protocol. Or maybe the jogger in the park told them to act like it was a real emergency. But either way, I knew the perception of urgency would make Laureen feel better.

Once Simba was loaded onto the gurney and whisked inside, I pulled out my wallet and handed Muhammad four twenty-dollar bills. "Hey, thanks," I said. "I know you didn't have to do this. And I realize it might get you into trouble with your company. But, believe me, I really appreciate it."

"No, no, no. It's okay," said Muhammad, waving off the money. "No charge for this ride. I am very sorry about your dog."

"Take it," I said. "You haven't seen the backseat yet. You're going to have some cleaning up to do."

"No, really, sir. I don't want your money," he said. But I took the crumpled bills and thrust them into his hand anyway, which was probably the wrong thing to do, but at that point, I was in a hurry and not really thinking straight.

Then I ran inside.

I passed through two sets of automatic doors into the small first-floor lobby. Laureen was talking to the woman behind the front desk. She sent us up to the third floor, where we checked in at another desk and filled out some forms. After that, we sat in the waiting room, holding hands and not saying much. Ten minutes later, Angela and Grace emerged from the elevator, looking upset, and Angela said, "What's going on, Mommy? Is Simba okay?"

"We don't know yet," said Laureen.

Five more minutes passed, then ten, and I began to envision a miracle. "Okay, he looked dead to me," I thought. "But, hey, I'm not a veterinarian. Maybe they have some way to bring him back to life—like with those electric paddles or something. Maybe there's a chance after all."

Ten more minutes passed. And with every passing minute, I became just a tiny bit more optimistic.

"Do you think there's any chance he might live?" asked Laureen.

"They've been in there an awfully long time," I replied, "so maybe there is."

"I think there is," she said.

A few more minutes passed and a young woman in blue scrubs came in holding a clipboard. I didn't know whether she was a veterinarian or a nurse. She glanced around the waiting room and said, "Simba? Simba?"

Laureen, Angela, Grace, and I all stood up.

"Are you Simba's family?" she asked.

"Yes," I replied. "We're Simba's family."

She paused for a moment. It seemed like a long time. Then she said, in a kind-but-practiced way. "I'm sorry, but Simba passed away. We believe he had a heart attack. We did everything we could to revive him. But it was too late. I'm very sorry for your loss."

Laureen still wasn't crying, but she was close.

"Would you like to see him?" the woman asked. The girls just looked stunned. And Laureen said, "Yes. We want to say good-bye."

The woman ushered us down a hallway and into a small examination room where Simba was laid out on a metal table. His eyes were still open, so he didn't look like he was sleeping. He just looked vacant, empty—like our faithful old buddy in form and substance but without the spark of life.

Laureen approached Simba first. She cradled his head and, for the first time since he collapsed in the park, she let herself break down. For her, Simba was yet another loved one in a long line of family members, close friends, and pets who had died and left her behind—her mother from breast cancer when Laureen was only ten; her beloved stepbrother from colon cancer when she was in college; then Simba the First, again from cancer; and after that, her father and her best friend.

"Thank you, Simba," she said through her tears. "Thank you for being such a good dog. Thank you for being part of our family."

"You were the best dog ever," said Angela, tears streaming down her cheeks.

Some might say that Simba's sudden death was the worst possible welcome to our new home in New York. And most of the time, when I tell people the story, that's their first reaction. But I disagree, because our first encounter with New Yorkers in a time of sorrow and vulnerability was characterized by authentic compassion, subtle discretion, and a wholehearted willingness to help out a couple of complete strangers.

I mean, really, how could any random group of people have been kinder, more sensitive, or more generous of spirit? Two people we never met carried an eighty-five-pound dog a quarter of a mile through Central Park. Two others gently placed him inside a taxi. The cabby, who rushed Simba to the hospital didn't want to be paid for the ride. And craziest of all—I mean really crazy—a group of eight or ten people—none of whom knew each other—resolved without a word, to maintain the fiction that Simba could still be saved in order to spare Laureen's feelings. Even the guy in the plaid shirt called me at the animal hospital like he said he would—just to make sure we were all right.

Once when I told a lifelong New Yorker how a random group of Manhattanites reacted so compassionately when our dog passed away in Central Park, he replied very knowingly, "Yeah, New

Yorkers are great on the little stuff, the stuff that doesn't require any real effort."

But to our family, Simba's death and the compassion we received wasn't little stuff. It was big stuff. So to those of you who say New York is a cold, hard city full of heartless people who only care about themselves, I say fuhgeddaboutit. Because the very first group of New Yorkers we encountered on a hot Sunday afternoon in Central Park, well, they all pitched in when we really needed it. Those are the New York values we saw. And now we couldn't be prouder to call ourselves New Yorkers.

I actually have a theory about the natural kindness of the New Yorkers you meet on the street and in the shops every day. But let me preface it by saying that even though I'm from little Erie, Pennsylvania, I didn't just fall off the turnip truck. And I do realize that not every single citizen of this great metropolis is a kindhearted angel—not by a long shot. Anytime you pack more than eight million people into a relatively small space, you're going to get a fair number of jerks and a smaller group of truly heinous human beings. But that being said, I contend that New Yorkers on whole are a generally kind and friendly people—much more so than when I left dirty, belligerent, crime-plagued Manhattan for supposedly mellow, wear-some-flowers-in-your-hair San Francisco back in 1988.

So what happened over the course of the last three decades to change the basic human nature of a sprawling metropolis? Personally I think this sea change dates back to the World Trade Center attack in 2001. On that horrific autumn morning, New Yorkers— young and old, rich and poor, brown, black, and white—were all united by a common enemy and deeply moved both by the terrible loss of life and by the sacrifice made by more than four-hundred first responders who died in the service of their fellow New Yorkers. Compassion was the silver lining of that unspeakable act. And amazingly, this sense that we're all in this thing together seems to have persisted for well over a decade.

And while I would like to think that a similar small group of super-liberal, affluent Marin County residents or the strutting young techno-lords of Silicon Valley would have reacted to Simba's death in the same spectacularly kind and sensitive manner, it's honestly hard to imagine. It's far more difficult to build and maintain a sense of camaraderie and compassion for your neighbor when you haven't lived through a shared disaster. And it's even more difficult when all of your neighbors live behind high hedges and zoom past each other in Teslas and Priuses all day. As odd as it sounds, my new Manhattan neighborhood, Carnegie Hill, feels more like a small town to me—a place where the kids in their various uniforms and blazers all walk to school in the morning, people in the shops know your name, and the many, many folks walking their dogs early in the morning and late at night readily converse with each other on the sidewalk.

Another reaction I get when I tell people the story of Simba's death is that it's a shame he died only minutes after arriving in his new hometown. But again, I respectfully disagree. Simba got to see his family one more time before he died. He reveled in our warm embrace. And he heard every one of us tell him, from the bottom of our hearts, just how much we loved and cherished him. And I believe from the bottom of my own heart that old Simba, through sheer dint of will, held death at bay until he could say good-bye to Laureen and the girls, but most of all, Laureen. Of course, there's no way to prove that. And it's pretty easy to poke holes in the theory. Like how would Simba even know that Laureen and the girls were waiting for him? Or how far we had to go before he could see them?

So let me put it another way. If you tell me it's a shame Simba died the way he did, I would tell you that when we stopped in Pittsburgh to visit my mother, I saw what a bad death looked like. A bad death is a two-year-long, dread-ridden slide toward oblivion where every day is incrementally worse than the day before it and slightly better than every day to come. A bad death is lying in a shadowy room drugged up and tethered to an oxygen machine in constant fear of suffocation. A bad death is being cut off from the world.

Simba's death wasn't a bad death. It was a good death. In fact, I would go so far as to say that it was a poetic death. Saying good-bye to your beloved family, romping around Central Park on a sunny late-summer afternoon with a bunch of other dogs, and then kicking the bucket in under a minute? I don't think it gets any better than that.

In fact, Simba's death and our journey across America gave me a new way of thinking about death and dying as I bid middle age adieu and look sixty squarely in the eye. It's not a particularly complex or profound theory. But it works for me, and it goes like this: Life is basically a crapshoot. And you never really know how long you will live or what effect your life might have on the lives of others or the world at large.

You might, for example, try to scam the rubes like Reverend Springer of Zzyzx, California, and end up saving a species of fish. You might raise $2 billion to build a solar farm that mitigates the effect of climate change and end up incinerating thousands of birds. You might go broke digging twenty-three years for a giant iron meteorite that was never there and end up advancing humankind's understanding of meteor strikes. You might half bury ten old Cadillacs in a Texas cow pasture as a wry commentary on American culture (or whatever) and end up delighting hundreds of thousands of visitors who neither know nor particularly care about your underlying message. You might write a song that inadvertently saves a town. Or dream of stardom, achieve it beyond your wildest dreams, and still die fat, lonely, and addicted on your cold bathroom floor.

The point is that, even though you should always act with good intentions—because, it's actually the road to heaven, not hell, that's paved with good intentions—you never know what the ultimate effect of those intentions will be. The only thing you know for sure is that someday you will die. You may go sooner or you may go later, but you will die. You can jog, do Pilates, go vegan, and avoid cholesterol, gluten, and dairy, but you will die nonetheless. You can get yourself the best doctors and the best drugs in the world and devote your life to avoiding any sort of physical risk. You can date young girls, buy a Porsche, dye your hair, and get Botoxed, all to forefend the onset of decrepitude. But you will still, most assuredly, die.

So maybe what we should hope and pray for is not the circumvention of death nor its unnatural deferment. Believe me, based on my mother's experience, the few extra months or years you get may not be worth it. Maybe what we should hope and pray for is a good death, a death like Simba's—the warm embrace of our family, a carefree romp in the golden sun, then a nice dump in the park before we shuffle off our mortal coil.

On a cold and rainy October evening, two months after Simba passed away, Angela, Grace, and Kara sat on the L-shaped sofa in the family room of our new apartment munching tortilla chips and staring mindlessly at *Law &Order: SVU*. Earlier that day, Laureen and I discreetly told Kara what we were up to. And what we were up to was picking up our brand new eight-week-old, seven-pound, fawn-colored pug puppy.

The new puppy, named Chang by his breeder, had huge black coffee-colored eyes, a black muzzle, black ears, and an adorable inch-wide black stripe around his tightly curled tail. Little Chang trembled on my lap as we drove back to Manhattan. When we got to the garage, Laureen grabbed his crate from the back seat. I wrapped him in a blanket and carried him in my arms around the corner to our apartment building. Then we took the elevator up four floors and entered the apartment as quietly as possible. When we got to the family room, I said, "Hey, Angela, look! I have a new friend for you—just like we promised."

Angela glanced up from her TV program and her jaw dropped. She squealed and yelled, "Oh my god, a pug, a pug! I can't believe there's a pug puppy in the house!

I handed the trembling little ball of fur over to Angela. And she hugged him and kissed him again and again before she reluctantly relinquished him to Grace, who gently stroked his tiny head. When it was Kara's turn to hold the new puppy, she immediately began to weep.

"Hey, why are you crying?" I asked Kara, who has always been quick to tears.

"He's so small and scared," she sobbed. "And he probably misses his family. I just feel sorry for him."

"Don't worry," I said. "He's going to have a pretty good life here."

"What should we name him?" asked Grace.

"Well, first of all, we're not going to name him Simba III," I replied. "So don't even think about it. We're retiring that name once and for all—like they retire the numbers of great ballplayers. Also, the breeder already named him Chang. We don't have to keep that name. He probably doesn't even know it's his name yet. But for some reason, I actually kind of like it."

"Isn't that racist?" asked Grace, who had attended a very politically correct girls' school in San Francisco for eight years and was therefore exquisitely sensitive in matters of gender, race, and sexual orientation.

"I don't know. Maybe." I replied, "Would you think it was racist if a Chinese family got a Labrador puppy and named him Max? Or if we named a French poodle Pierre? The pug is a Chinese breed. So maybe it's appropriate."

Over the course of the next several weeks, we discussed dog names over every family dinner. And we tried out a few to see how they felt. Angela, who loves the study of history and has always had a distinctly pedantic bent, wanted to name the new puppy Zheng He, after a fourteenth-century Chinese explorer who led an expeditionary fleet across the Indian Ocean to the east coast of Africa. Zheng He was a Chinese eunuch—like Chang would be in a few months—so they had that in common. But since no one in the family could pronounce "Zheng He" to Angela's satisfaction, it was a nonstarter—although Angela kept beating that horse for a while.

Grace, on the other hand, wanted to name the puppy something safe and straightforward like Budsy or Spud. But baby Chang seemed far too sweet and sensitive to shoulder such a backslapping sobriquet. So that didn't work.

Kara wanted to name him Gizmo because he looked like a creature with that name in an old eighties movie called *Gremlins*. But my personal favorite—also from Kara—was Voldemort, which seemed both ironic and appropriate because, like Harry Potter's evil nemesis, pugs have tiny smooshed-in noses, which, by the way, is where the term "pug nose" comes from.

But then, we took the puppy out for walks every day, and the various doormen in our building would ask his name, and we would all answer, "We're not sure yet, but for now we're calling him Chang." And since the doormen are trained to address every resident of the building by their formal name, they started calling the little fellow Mister Chang.

I'm not exactly sure why this archaic policy would extend to our dog. They didn't call Louis, the beagle, Mister Louis, or Charlie, the miniature poodle, Miss Charlie, to name just two of the twenty-five dogs that currently reside in our building. I guess it's probably because Chang is generally a surname and therefore requires an honorific. But whatever the reason, Chang became Mister Chang and Mister Chang stuck—although for the first three months we had him, Grace told everyone she met on the street that his name was Spud.

In many ways, Mister Chang was the polar opposite of our dear departed Simba. While Simba was a big strapping hound with a perpetual smile plastered across his gigantic face, Mister Chang was a barrel-shaped little nugget who always looked worried or grumpy—even when he wasn't. (The girls, using contemporary youth parlance, called his facial expression RBF for "Resting Bitch Face.") While Simba was an intrepid beast, more than happy to run off and explore the neighborhood for a few hours, Mister Chang was a sensitive soul who demanded and received constant attention and physical contact. And while Simba's favorite thing in the world was loping around the great outdoors splashing through mud puddles, Mister Chang either had to be forced or bribed with treats to leave the apartment at all—particularly during the frigid New York winter. And when we did finally get him out of the apartment and onto the street, he would prance down the avenue like a miniature dandy in his blue corduroy jacket, carefully avoiding every puddle and patch of snow on the sidewalk so he wouldn't get his precious little feet wet. And finally, while Simba devoted the greater part of his brain to thinking about food, Mister Chang seemed to crave affection above all else. As an older guy on the street once said to me, "Pugs are bred to love you. It's their survival strategy." That seems true, and I now understand why there are so many Crazy Pug People in the world.

Basically, Laureen and I treat Mister Chang more like a grandson than a pet, indulging his every desire. He sleeps in bed with us, or with one of the girls—something we would have never dreamed of letting Simba do. And believe me, I'm in no way proud of this, but after a few months we bowed to Mister Chang's unrelenting demands and added another chair to the dinner table so he could sit with us as an equal. So, yeah, now we're Crazy Pug People, too.

Oh, and one other thing. Although his breed is not particularly noted for this behavior, Mister Chang, bless his tiny Pug heart, absolutely loves to fetch little balls and dog toys—like Simba, the so-called Labrador retriever, never would—provided, of course, that he can do it inside the apartment.

On November 7, 2014, I received a late-night phone call from my mother.

"I'm not going to make it," she said hoarsely.

"What do you mean?" I replied in my groggy two-in-the-morning voice.

"I'm in the hospital," she replied, "and I'm going to die soon. So I wanted to call you and tell you that I love you and that you've always been a good son and that I'm very proud of you."

I told her I loved her, too. Then I assured her, very matter of factly, that she was not going to die, because first of all this wasn't the first time she'd called to say she was going to die. It was maybe the fourth or fifth time. And secondly, she'd already been in and out of the hospital three times in the last year without dying. And third of all, because that's what people always say in these situations, whether it's true or not. But after I hung up I realized that this was the first time my mother had called me in the middle of the night to tell me she was dying. So just in case, I groggily pulled out my iPad and booked a flight to Pittsburgh that would leave LaGuardia at eleven in the morning and arrive a little after noon.

But that turned out to be too late. Because this time my mother was right. And a few hours after she called me, her long-suffering cardiologist, Dr. Kross, bent over her hospital bed and said, "Hannah, there's nothing else I can do for you. I'll see you in heaven."

And my mother, rest her soul, gazed up at Dr. Kross—who had cared for her as if she were his own mother for more than five years—and said, "Dr. Kross, I don't think you're going to heaven."

Given her proclivity in recent years for pissing everyone off, my mother's funeral was surprisingly well attended—by more than a hundred mourners. Even Dr. Kross came. My brother, a Pittsburgh city councilman for twelve years—so very adept at public speaking—delivered a beautiful eulogy. Then I got up and tried to read a parable

I wrote about a mahogany-framed full-length mirror that was in my parent's apartment and in my childhood home before that.

It was an old mirror, and my mother used to admire herself in it back when she was young and beautiful. But very slowly, over the course of three decades—starting at the edges and moving toward the center—my mother covered the mirror with dozens of three-by-five photos of her eight grandchildren. So as her beauty faded, she saw less of herself reflected in the mirror and saw herself instead, as beautiful as ever, reflected in the faces of her grandchildren.

It was a very short eulogy, only a few minutes long, so I thought I could make it all the way through it without choking up. But it turned out I couldn't. So Laureen, who stood next to me at the dais, holding my hand, took over and delivered the last few sentences.

I was touched beyond words that Erick and his wife, Lisa, flew all the way from California on short notice. And they brought our other close friends from Marin, Yury and Zhenya, with them. And being proper Russians, Yury and Zhenya brought a half-gallon of vodka with them to the Shiva—which is sort of like a Jewish wake, only a lot less fun. And the vodka, which we drank in a series of shots over the long course of the mournful evening, allowed us to enjoy a truly bizarre moment that occurred when a female friend of my brother walked up to me at what was essentially my mother's wake and said, "I heard about your dog, and I'm very sorry for your loss."

I mean it was a nice sentiment and all. But it did seem an odd occasion to bring up Simba. And smart aleck that I am, I replied, "Yep. First the dog and now my mother." And while that may not sound funny to you now—probably because you haven't slammed enough vodka shots—it somehow struck Erick, Lisa, Yury, Zhenya, and me as hilarious, particularly when she walked away, and Lucas said, "Can we get a tiny Chinese grandma now?"

On a sunny New Year's Day, at the dawn of 2015, we held our own very small funeral for Simba. There was never any doubt where we would do it. The Sea Ranch on the rocky California coast was always Simba's favorite place on Earth. And anywhere else would have been entirely inappropriate.

Angela, Grace, Laureen, and I drove two-and-a-half hours up the coastal highway to Sea Ranch and pulled into our driveway. Then we walked through the house and straight out the back door to the cliff high above the crashing Pacific breakers. We each spoke for a few minutes about what Simba meant to us as a friend and companion and as an essential member of our family. Erick, who would soon get his own Labrador puppy, emailed a poem, "A Dog on His Master," by Billy Collins, which we read on his behalf. And after I read the poem, I wiggled open the rectangular tin box that held Simba's ashes, knelt down, and carefully poured them over the cliff toward the ocean thirty feet below. The ashes floated momentarily on the breeze and landed in a shallow tide pool. Then a wave rolled in and out again carrying Simba's earthly remains out to sea.

I don't remember exactly what I said during my brief tribute to Simba II, the wrong dog at the beginning of this story but undeniably the right dog at the end. But I now know what I should have said. Because when I got back to New York, I had lunch with my old friend Greenie, who is a terrific photojournalist and a great guy who has faced down a lot of adversity in his life. After lunch, as Greenie and I rode in a cab up Madison Avenue to my apartment, I told him the story of Simba's journey across America and his remarkable demise in Central Park.

And when I finished the story, Greenie turned to me and said, "You know I have a little Yorkie named Brutus. And I love him just as much as you loved Simba. And you know what I realized? I realized that we don't love our dogs because they give us unconditional love—even though that's what everyone says. We love our dogs because they show us that we, ourselves, are capable of loving another being unconditionally."

So yeah, that's what I should have said at Simba's funeral. I should have said, "Simba, you loved us unconditionally. And more importantly, we loved you unconditionally. And how precious is that in this dog-eat-dog world?"

Wow. It's been five years since *The Wrong Dog* was published and nearly seven years since Erick, Simba, and I embarked on our cross-country journey. I mentioned near the end of *The Wrong Dog* that several months after Simba passed away, we adopted a tiny, eight-week-old pug. His previous owner named the little guy Chang. Then the doormen in our New York City apartment building changed that to Mr. Chang. And finally, when he received his therapy dog certificate, everyone started calling him Dr. Chang.

The name still embarrasses our children, who consider it vaguely racist. But in some ways Dr. Chang is an apt moniker. I don't mean to cast aspersions on the late, great Simba, who will always hold a singular place in our hearts, but Dr. Chang turned out to be—and I don't know how to say this diplomatically—a much smarter dog. Like Einstein smart. No, more like Bond villain smart. While Simba was a big, loping aristocratic goofball who loved long walks through nature and splashing through ponds and mud puddles, Dr. Chang is a prissy intellectual who prances around even the smallest puddle on a New York City sidewalk and won't go out in the rain unless it's an absolute emergency.

Dr. Chang knows when the corner pet store is open for business, and he drags me over there to get a treat from the cashier during every two o'clock walk. But he doesn't bother during his early morning and late evening walks because, somehow, he knows that the pet store will be closed. He also knows the difference between the sound my iPhone makes when someone calls me and the sound it makes when someone rings our front doorbell, which is a sort of intercom. When it's the intercom, he runs to the door and barks, fulfilling his sacred duty to guard the perimeter. But if it's a phone call, he just stays put on the couch.

Dr. Chang sits at the dinner table in a chair like the other members of the family—and as I said in *The Wrong Dog*, we're not particularly proud of that. But he knows that he'll be banished to the floor like a normal dog if he ever whines or barks for food. So when Dr. Chang sees something he particularly wants to eat, he softly bangs his paw on the table three times like a tiny Khrushchev. And that, of course, is so funny that we usually give it to him.

Perhaps most impressively—and I don't expect you to believe me, but I swear it's true—Dr. Chang has somehow worked out the relationship between passports and international travel. If he sees Laureen's passport lying on our bed or inside her open briefcase, he knows she'll be leaving home for a while. He doesn't like that, so he takes matters into his own paws. The first time it happened, Laureen was supposed to visit American Express's law offices in Mexico. Dr. Chang saw the passport inside her open bag, removed it, and chewed it to the point where she had to delay her trip and get a new passport from the State Department on an emergency basis.

We thought that might be a coincidence, that maybe he just wanted something to gnaw on. I mean he is, after all, a dog. But then a year later, when Laureen was supposed to go to Hong Kong with her CEO for an American Express board meeting, Dr. Chang grabbed her passport from on top of the bed. And when it came time for Laureen to leave, the passport was nowhere to be found. Laureen called the CEO and told him he better go without her, that she would somehow catch up to him. Then she spent the next twelve hours exhaustively searching our apartment from top to bottom. Laureen couldn't find the passport anywhere, but she did find more than twenty chew bones and miscellaneous stuffed animals that Dr. Chang had secreted under beds, behind radiators, and under couch cushions in pretty much every room in the apartment.

Once again, Laureen had to call the State Department, and she made it to the board meeting with literally two minutes to spare. The passport turned up seven weeks later when Grace was walking through our family room barefoot and noticed a slight lump under one corner of the rug. Dr. Chang had somehow stashed the passport between the wool rug and the rubber pad beneath it. Laureen had looked under the pad, but not between the pad and the rug. Now we make sure that our passports are never in plain view.

So like I said, Dr. Chang is an evil genius. And he seems to understand more than fifty English phrases including:

- "Do you want your din-din?" (He runs to his bowl.)
- "Stay here, I'll be right back." (He stays put.)

- "Do you want go to the beach?" (He runs to the car.)
- And most importantly, to him at least, "Do you want to go to the pet store?" (At which point, he runs to the front door.)

But Dr. Chang also shares the many endearing breed traits of a pug, which means that if you sit down in a chair, he immediately jumps up on your lap. If you lie down on the couch, he creeps between your legs. Every night, he burrows under our covers and proceeds to snore loudly. And if I'm at home, he's never more than two feet away. All this, of course, is very charming and more than makes up for his diabolical ploys. In fact, everyone in the house wants to snuggle with Dr. Chang all the time. This has given rise to the term "pug-jacking," which means that someone (usually one of the girls) will run into the room and grab the dog from someone else, so she can curl up with him. Pug-jacking ran rampant during the recent pandemic, when the younger girls were home from college for a year and a half and Kara and her husband stayed with us for several months. All during that difficult time, Dr. Chang was a source of snuggly comfort, and he provided solace to everyone in the house.

I know that someday, Dr. Chang, like Simba before him, will cross the rainbow bridge. As the late great comedian George Carlin famously said, "Every pet is a small tragedy waiting to happen." But I take comfort in the fact that unlike Labs and other large dogs, pugs often live well into their teens. And there was, supposedly, a South African pug named Snookie who lived well into his twenties. I don't know about that, but I have personally met an eighteen-year-old pug, gamely limping down the sidewalk in New York. Mr. Chang is only seven, and I'm in my mid-sixties now. So who knows? Maybe I'll be spared Chang's demise and someday he'll say goodbye to me.

NOTES

Chapter 1

13   "Animal Fighting Case Study: Michael Vick," The Animal Legal Defense Fund, aldf.org, last revised January 2011.

Chapter 4

37   http://dogs.wikia.com/wiki/Labrador_Retriever.

40   "Hunter-Gatherers to Farmers, The Neolithic Revolution: 10,000 years ago," www.historyworld.net.

      "Origin of Domestic Dogs," by Ed Yong, *The Scientist*, November 14, 2013.

      Geronticide: Killing the Elderly, by Mike Brogden, Jessica Kingsley Publishers, 2001, pp. 60-61.

Chapter 7

76   www.sftodo.com/sanfranciscoweather.

77   *Legendary Route 66: A Journey Through Time Along America's Mother Road*, by Michael Karl Witzel and Gyvel Young-Witzel, 2007, Voyageur Press.

      "History of the Bakersfield Sound," by Jeff Nickell, first printed in the Spring 2002 issue of *Historic Kern*, Kern County Historical Society. Reprinted at www.visitbakersfield.com/visitors/attractions/history-bakersfield-sound/

      "Bonnie Owens, 76; Singer and Ex-Wife of 2 Country Stars," by Steve Chawkins, *Los Angeles Times*, April 26, 2006.

Chapter 8

88   www.usacitiesonline.com.

      "World's largest thermometer repaired in California," *USA Today*, July 11, 2014.

90   *Weird California: Your Travel Guide to California's Local Legends and Best Kept Secrets*, by Greg Bishop, Joe Oesterle, Mike Marinacci, Mark Moran and Mark Sceurman, Sterling, 2006.

      Much of this information in this section comes from an article entitled "Quack-Founded Town With Last Name in the Alphabet," at www.roadsideamerica.com.

92   "Curtis Springer's Last Appearance at Zzyzx," KNBC, Los Angeles, 1974, www.youtube.com.

93   "The $2.2 Billion Bird-Scorching Solar Project," by Cassandra Sweet, *The Wall Street Journal*, February, 12, 2014.

      "Ivanpah thermal solar power plant produces 'death rays' torching many birds," by Ralph Maughan, *The Wildlife News*, August 24, 2014, and "'Alarming' Rate Of Bird Deaths As New Solar Plants Scorch Animals In Mid-Air," by Ellen Knickmeyer and John Locher, Associated Press, August 18, 2014.

Chapter 9

105   bulletsandburgers.com.

106   www.tripadvisor.com/Attraction_Review-g45963-d3697929-Reviews-Bullets_and_Burgers-Las_Vegas_Nevada.

Chapter 10

114 "Landmark speaks volumes. A few critics aside, residents of Effingham are proud to claim the largest cross in the United States," by Ted Gregory, *Chicago Tribune*, May 21, 2002.

http://www.crossministries.net.

116 "Disaster for Barringer," www.barringercrater.com/about/history_5.php.

118 *Gazetteer of Planetary Nomenclature* by the International Astronomical Union (IAU), Working Group for Planetary System Nomenclature (WGPSN), http://planetarynames.wr.usgs.gov/Feature/616.

"Earth Impact Database," University of New Brunswick.

122 "'Take It Easy' by Eagles," www.songfacts.com/detail.php?id=3067.

standinonthecorner.com/park-history.

124 http://artofjohnpugh.com/murals/

"Standin' on the Corner Park," www.roadsideamerica.com/story/12603.

128 "Geology and the Painted Desert," National Park Service, U.S. Department of the Interior, http://www.nps.gov/pefo/upload/Geology2006.pdf.

"CO_2 as a primary driver of Phanerozoic climate" by Dana L. Royer and Robert A. Berner, Isabel P. Montañez, Neil J. Tabor and David J. Beerling, *GSA Today*, volume 14, number 3, pages 4-10.

"What Is Petrified Wood? How Does It Form?" http://geology.com/stories/13/petrified-wood/

129   "Petrified Forest National Park,"
      http://travel.nationalgeographic.com/travel/national-parks/
      petrified-forest-national-park/

      "Arizona's Petrified Forest Is Stealing Away," by Charles
      Hillinger, *The Los Angeles Times*, August 5, 1990.

130   "Petrified Forest Shrinks, One Stolen Piece at a Time," *The
      New York Times*, November 28, 1999, and "Rocks with a
      conscience pile up at Petrified Forest," by Larry Hendricks,
      azdailysun.com, October 27, 2012.

      "Civilian Conservation Corps (CCC),"
      http://www.nps.gov/pefo/learn/historyculture/ccc.htm.

Chapter 11

135   According to the census bureau, McKinley County's poverty
      rate is 35%, which is 2.5 times the national average. From
      "McKinley County, New Mexico," quickfacts.census.gov/
      qfd/states/35/35031.

      http://www.greatamericanstations.com/Stations/GLP.

      "History of Gallup," www.gallupnm.gov.

      "U.S. to pay Navajo Nation $554 million in largest
      settlement with single Indian tribe," by Sari Horowitz, *The
      Washington Post*, September 24, 2014.

136-137 "A Town's Showdown With Problem Drinking. Step-By-
      Step, Gallup, N.M., Is Mending Its Reputation," by Gwen
      Florio, *Philadelphia Inquirer*, February 27, 1999.

      Ibid, Florio.

      tribalemployee.blogspot.com.

"Health Highlight Report for McKinley County,"
https://ibis.health.state.nm.us/community/highlight/report/
geocnty/31.html.

"New Mexico leads nation in alcohol-related deaths," by
Patrick Malone, *The Santa Fe New Mexican*, July 7, 2014.

"Rash of exposure deaths in Gallup, N.M., blamed on an
old foe: Alcoholism," by Nigel Duara, *Los Angeles Times*,
April 8, 2015.

137   http://blog.credit.com/2013/09/poorest-cities-in-america/

http://www.city-data.com/crime/crime-Gallup-New-Mexico.
html.

138   "Gallup named Most Patriotic Small Town," Associated
Press, October 11, 2013.

"The Navajo Nation's Own 'Trail Of Tears,'"
http://www.npr.org/2005/06/15/4703136/the-navajo-
nation's-own-trail-of-tears.

http://www.bosqueredondomemorial.com.

146   "Betty Hutton buried in small ceremony," Associated Press,
March 13, 2007.

Chapter 12

151   "Doug Michels, Radical Artist and Architect, Dies at 59," by
Ken Johnson, *The New York Times*, June 21, 2003.

"Beilue: Cadillac Ranch turns 40: Ant Farm artists, Marsh
make lasting icon," by Jon Mark Beilue, *Amarillo Globe-
News*, June 29, 2014.

152   "Stanley Marsh 3's letter to Ant Farm artists on the Cadillac
Ranch proposal," by Jon Mark Beilue, *Amarillo Globe-News*,
June 29, 2014.

"Stanley Marsh, Cadillac Rancher, Dies at 76, Shadowed by Charges," by Bruce Weber, *The New York Times*, June 23, 2014.

Ibid, Weber.

153   Artist Hudson Marquez: "'Anybody Who Talks About Their Art is Like, Full of Shit'," by Jennifer Swann, *LA Weekly*, January 15, 2013.

http://mediaburn.org/video/media-burn-by-ant-farm-1975-edit/

Chapter 13

157   https://www.grammy.com/photos/roger-miller.

"The Life of Roger Miller (1936-1992)," www.rogermiller.com/bio3.

"Do-Wacka-Do," Roger Miller Museum Newsletter, 33rd Edition, September 2013, http://www.rogermillermuseum.com/newsletter.html.

158   "The Life of Roger Miller (1936-1992)," www.rogermiller.com/bio1.

"Erick, Oklahoma," at Sperling's Best Places, www.bestplaces.net.

160   "McVeigh Chronology, Frontline," www.pbs.org/wgbh/pages/frontline/documents/mcveigh/mcveigh3.

"FAQs about the Memorial Grounds," home.nps.gov/okci/sitefaqs.htm.

"Inside McVeigh's mind," by Robin Aitken, news.bbc.co.uk, June 11, 2001.

161 "The Shadow of Waco," *New York Times* video, July 15, 2015.

"Waco: The Inside Story, Frequently Asked Questions, Janet Reno Statement," www.pbs.org/wgbh/pages/frontline//renoopeningst.

"Sacred and Profane," by Malcolm Gladwell, *The New Yorker*, March 31, 2014.

"Waco: The Inside Story, Chronology of the Siege," www.pbs.org/wgbh/pages/frontline/waco/timeline.

162 "Profile: Timothy McVeigh," news.bbc.co.uk, May 11, 2001.

Ibid, BBC.

163 "Trooper who arrested Timothy McVeigh shares story," by Kim Morava, *The Shawnee News-Star*, February 25, 2009.

"Okla. families can watch McVeigh execution on TV," by Terry Frieden, cnn.com, April 12, 2001.

"Oklahoma City National Memorial," www.nps.gov.

Chapter 14

173 "Building the Center," https://www.clintonfoundation.org.

178 "Elvis Presley jets for sale amid Graceland makeover," by Alan Duke, cnn.com, September 1, 2014.

"Elvis Presley's Graceland: 3764 Elvis Presley Boulevard," graceland.elvis.com.au.

180 "Elvis at Graceland," at www.graceland.com.

Elvis Presley: The Man. The Life. The Legend, by Pamela Clarke Keogh, Simon & Schuster, 2008, page 2.

"7 Fascinating Facts about Elvis Presley," by Elizabeth Nix, www.history.com, July 1, 2014.

181 *Elvis Cinema and Popular Culture* by Douglas Brode, McFarland & Co., 2006, p. 21.

"Elvis Presley in Germany," http://www.german-way.com.

"Elvis Presley's Charitable Acts," elvis.wikia.com.

182 A Rare Chat With Colonel Parker," *The Chicago Tribune*, August 14, 1989.

"When Elvis Met Nixon," by Peter Carlson, *Smithsonian Magazine*, December 2010.

"Elvis uncovered," by Ray Connolly, *Daily Mail*, undated, retrieved July 17, 2015.

ACKNOWLEDGMENTS

My sincere thanks to:

Publishing guru Michael Fragnito for his sage advice and friendship

My smart and faithful agent of twenty-five years, Carol Mann

My wonderful publisher, Lisa McGuinness

My longtime co-designer and digital pre-press genius, Peter Truskier

My brilliant readers: Barbara Berger, Jeff Epstein, Mark Greenberg, Angela Seeger, and Joe Sweeney

My saintly father, Norman Cohen

My steadfast brother and sister-in-law, Dan and Stacey Cohen

… and most of all, my beloved Laureen, Kara, Will, Lucas, Angela, and Grace

… and, of course, the noble Simba (2000–14)

The Wrong Dog is dedicated to my mother,
Hannah M. Cohen
(1930–2014)

Wedding Day: Laureen and I tie the knot in Napa Valley on August 19, 2006. *Doug Menuez*

Handsome Boy: Simba, age six, in November 2006. *Michael Hornbogen*

Once Upon a Time: My mother,
Hannah, (above) in the late 1960s; my father,
Norm, (above, right) at Fort Bragg in 1945 and with Kara.

Best Friends: Simba and Grace, age seven, October 10, 2006.

Michael Hornbogen

Blended Family: Simba, age 8, with (clockwise) Lucas, 15; Kara, 21; Will, 20; Angela, 12; and Grace, 10 on August 22, 2009. *Michael Hornbogen*

Road Warriors: Erick, Simba, and I pose for a photo in Erick's driveway before leaving on our cross-country journey. *Lisa Miller*

Mojave Heat: According to the "world's tallest thermometer," it was 111° in aptly named Baker, California. *Erick Steinberg*

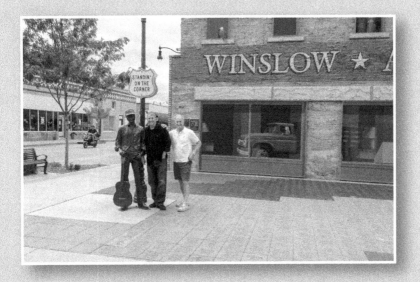

Takin' It Easy: Paying homage to the classic Eagles hit at Standin' on the Corner Park in Winslow, Arizona.

Painted Desert: Erick taking photos at Petrified Forest National Park.
David Elliot Cohen

Painted Cars:
Simba (above)
relaxes at Cadillac
Ranch near
Amarillo, Texas.
Erick Steinberg

Erick in Erick:
Erick fulfills a
childhood dream by
visiting his namesake
town in Oklahoma.
David Elliot Cohen

Ashes to Ashes: Grace holds Simba's ashes at Sea Ranch before I drop them thirty feet off a cliff into the Pacific Ocean on January 1, 2015. *David Elliot Cohen*

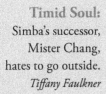

Timid Soul:
Simba's successor,
Mister Chang,
hates to go outside.
Tiffany Faulkner

ABOUT THE AUTHOR

For three decades, bestselling author and editor David Elliot Cohen has created books that have sold six million copies worldwide. Most were in the immensely popular *Day in the Life* and *America 24/7* photography book series. A proud graduate of Yale University and Cathedral Preparatory School in Erie, Pennsylvania, Cohen has four *New York Times* bestsellers to his credit along with two other #1 bestsellers—in Australia and Spain. His 1999 memoir, *One Year Off*, was a national bestseller. He lives in Manhattan with his wife, Laureen Seeger, and the youngest of their five children—the other four having flown the nest.

yellow pear 🍐 press

Yellow Pear Press, established in 2015, publishes inspiring, charming, clever, distinctive, playful, imaginative, beautifully designed lifestyle books, cookbooks, literary fiction, notecards, and journals with a certain joie de vivre in both content and style. Yellow Pear Press books have been honored by the Independent Publisher Book (IPPY) Awards, National Indie Excellence Awards, Independent Press Awards, and International Book Awards. Reviews of our titles have appeared in Kirkus Reviews, Foreword Reviews, Booklist, Midwest Book Review, San Francisco Chronicle, and New York Journal of Books, among others. Yellow Pear Press joined forces with Mango Publishing in 2020, both with the vision to continue publishing clever and innovative books. The fact that they're both named after fruit is a total coincidence.

We love hearing from our readers, so please stay in touch with us and follow us at:

Facebook: Mango Publishing
Twitter: @MangoPublishing
Instagram: @MangoPublishing
LinkedIn: Mango Publishing
Pinterest: Mango Publishing
Newsletter: mangopublishinggroup.com/newsletter